Messiah's Alphabet

Word Study Series

Yeshua

Appearances of the name *Jesus* throughout the the Old Testament – and how the name's Hebrew roots are expressed in the New Testament

Messiah's Alphabet

Word Study Series

Yeshua

Appearances of the name *Jesus* throughout the the Old Testament – and how the name's Hebrew roots are expressed in the New Testament

James T. and Lisa M. Cummins

Indeed, then I will return my people to a pure language
so that they all may call upon the name of the Lord,
serving him with a united will.
Zephaniah 3:9, ISV

But the goal of our instruction is love from a pure heart
and a good conscience and a sincere faith.
1 Timothy 1:5, NASB

Contents

Contents, *continued*

Introduction

Introduction

Yeshua is just the Hebrew name for *Jesus*. *Yeshua* is His original name – the name He went by while walking the planet among humankind many centuries ago. As the good news of God's gift of salvation spread from one culture to another down through the centuries, the pronunciation of the name *Yeshua* changed slightly each time it got translated into a new language. This series of alterations eventually resulted in the English name *Jesus*.

Like all Biblical Hebrew names, the name *Yeshua* is formed from Hebrew words which have distinct meanings of their own. This workbook will explore the meanings of the two Hebrew words that make up the name *Yeshua*. We'll lead you through a brief word study which displays how the Hebrew roots of the name *Yeshua* are expressed throughout Scripture – all the way into the Greek New Testament. By the end of this little workbook, you will have a much clearer and deeper understanding of the varied and layered expressions of the meaning of the name *Yeshua*.

This workbook will also list all the instances of the name *Yeshua* exactly as it appears in the Hebrew Scriptures of the Bible. Yes, you read that right! **Contrary to popular belief, the name of Jesus actually appears in the TaNaCH (Hebrew Old Testament)!** (You may be surprised to learn that not just one man, but *many* different Israelites, bore this traditional Jewish name throughout Old Testament times.) We'll teach you how to recognize Yeshua's name in its original Hebrew spelling there.

If you've flipped through the pages of this workbook and noticed a bunch of foreign-looking letters throughout, please don't be alarmed. Some of what you see is Hebrew, and some is Greek. Those readers who happen to know the Hebrew and Greek alphabets will enjoy scanning the excerpts from the Scriptures in their original languages. However, we want to emphasize that **foreign language skills are <u>not</u> necessary for this study. You can still learn everything that this workbook has to offer, even with no prior Greek or Hebrew knowledge.** That's because we provide written pronunciations (called *transliterations*) of any foreign words you'll need to know. (To *transliterate* means to "spell out" the pronunciation of a foreign word using the letters of your own language. For example, the Hebrew word שָׁלוֹם might be transliterated *shalom*.) Also, we always provide the meaning (*translation*) of every foreign word, so that **the average English reader with no foreign language experience can easily understand every page of this text.**

So, you don't have to be an Einstein or a Rhodes scholar to enjoy this book. We promise to keep everything as simple and easy as possible. Our goal is that you be able to relax and enjoy the process of learning. We rely on the Holy Spirit to lead you into all truth as you search the Scriptures for the name *Yeshua* and discover its true Hebrew meaning. Remember that it's Jesus Himself who promises, "He who seeks shall find."

Before we begin, let's offer a prayer of thanksgiving to our LORD, Messiah Yeshua (Jesus the Christ) for the chance to study His glorious Hebrew name as it appears throughout the TaNaCH. "Thank You, LORD, for this wonderful opportunity! Amen!" Now. Are you ready to begin a wonderful adventure? Let's go!

Lesson 1

Why do we call Him "Jesus" instead of "Yeshua"?

Lesson 1:

Why do we call Him "Jesus" instead of "Yeshua"?

Whenever we teach Biblical Hebrew to a small group, we always take the time to introduce the Biblical Hebrew name for *Jesus*, which is יֵשׁוּעַ *Yeshua*. Technically, this Hebrew name is properly pronounced *yay-SHOO-ah*, although most of us Americans tend toward the lazier, less exact pronunciation of *yeh-SHOO-ah* or *y'SHOO-ah* in our speech habits.

As soon as we begin teaching about the origins of the name *Jesus* to any group of people, it never fails that we get the question, "But Jesus isn't actually a Hebrew name, is it? It's a Greek name, right?"

That's a very good question, and we can certainly see why our students ask it. After all, *Jesus* has that characteristically Greek ending of *-us*, just like the names *Theophilus* and *Alpheus*. And, when you look up the name *Jesus* in your concordance, you'll never find any Old Testament listings for that spelling. If *Jesus* is such a "good old" Hebrew name, then why isn't the TaNaCH[1] full of references to it?

The short answer is that the name *Yeshua* had to be slightly modified because of certain pronunciation and grammatical constraints in the Greek and Latin languages. Then, over many centuries, it became anglicized[2] in pronunciation. Rest assured, though: *Yeshua* in its Hebrew spelling (יֵשׁוּעַ) is indeed an ancient Hebrew name which can be found many places in the TaNaCH. Soon, we'll display all the instances of those Scripture verses in both Hebrew and English so that you'll be able to verify this fact for yourself.

Before we show you those verses, though, we should first let you see how the English language ended up with the spelling *Jesus* in the first place. Turn the page, and you'll see that the name has gone through quite a transformation!

---

1. **TaNaCH**: sometimes written *Tanakh* or *Tanach* (pronounced *tah-NAHKH* so that it rhymes with *Bach*) – the Jewish/Messianic term for what Gentile Christians call the Old Testament, i.e., all the Hebrew Scriptures of the Bible. *TaNaCH* is an acronym of the first Hebrew letter of each of the three traditional divisions of the Hebrew Scriptures: *Torah* ("Teaching," i.e., Genesis through Deuteronomy), *Nevi'im* ("Prophets") and *Ketuvim* ("Writings"). If you are a Gentile Christian, you might find it helpful to make a habit of mentally or even orally substituting the words "Old Testament" with "TaNaCH." Memorizing this term – and other such traditional Jewish terminology – will greatly help your future studies in Hebraic subjects. It will also facilitate any conversations you might have with traditional or orthodox Jewish people.

2. **anglicized**: made English in form or character. For example, early Greek immigrants to America sometimes anglicized their names from *Dionysios* to *Dennis* or from *Stavros* to *Steve*. French names were transformed from *Jacques* to *James* or from *Michel* to *Michael*. Italian names changed from *Antonio* to *Anthony* or from *Giuseppe* to *Joseph*. And traditional Jewish names couldn't escape the unrelenting force of anglicization, either. *Yitzchak* went from *Isaac* all the way to *Ike*. *Baruch* became *Barry*. *Yochanan* turned into *John*, *Miriam* to *Mary*, *Mattityahu* to *Matthew*, *Natan'el* to *Nate*, and *Shimon* to *Simon*, just to name a few.

How the name *Yeshua* changed into *Jesus* after being translated from language to language

The *Messiah's Alphabet* workbook series often uses cartoon characters in ethnic clothing to represent different languages. Next to each character, we display a scroll. The **scroll** shows how a word is **written** in that language. Coming from the character's mouth is a cartoon "speech bubble." The **speech bubble** shows how a word is **pronounced** in that language. We think you'll find this teaching method simple and effective (and we hope the cartoons make it fun, too). Let's watch as our cartoon characters take you through the story of the name *Yeshua*. It's a bit of a long story, so it will take several pages. Keep turning!

Our story begins with the Hebrew name *Y'hoshua*. This very old and apparently popular name was the name of Moses' successor and many other Israelites. Not familiar with *Y'hoshua*? That may be because most of our English Bible translations today spell it as *Jehoshua*, *Jehoshuah*, or *Joshua*. The name means "the Lord is salvation."

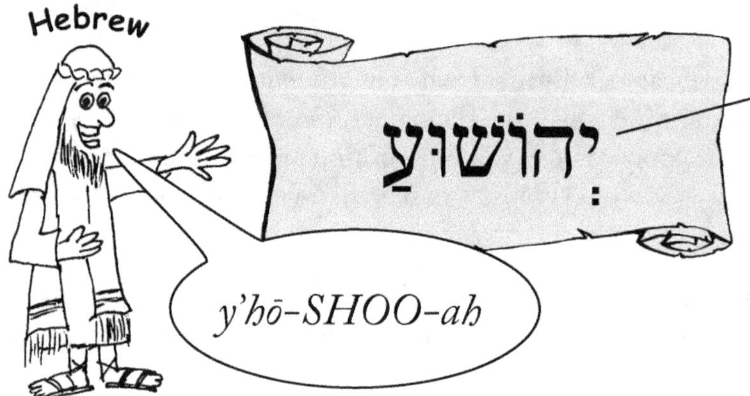

This is how the name is spelled in the Hebrew Scriptures, for example in Deuteronomy 3:21.

Over the centuries of Israel's history, names got shortened. By the time of Ezra, people had begun calling their sons by a short-form version of *Y'hoshua*: *Yeshua*. (Short-form names are common to all languages. English has *Rob* for *Robert* and *Bill* for *William*, for example.)

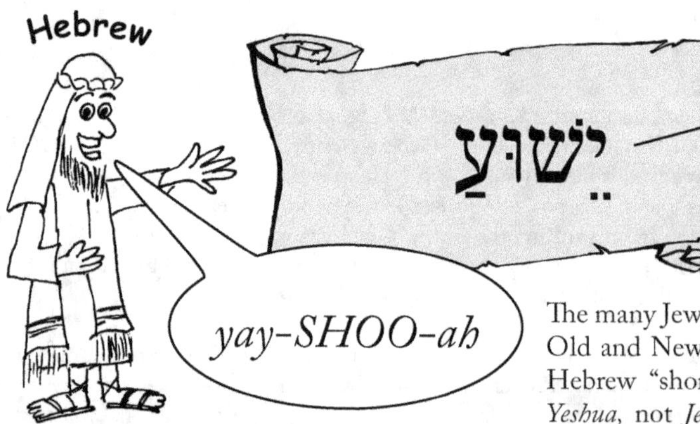

This is how the name is spelled in the Hebrew Scriptures, for example in Ezra 2:2.

The many Jewish men who bore the name of *Jesus* during Old and New Testament times were actually using this Hebrew "short-form version" of *Joshua* – pronounced *Yeshua*, not *Jesus*. Most English Old Testaments spell this name as *Jeshua*. Over the next few pages, we'll explain why they exchanged the Y for a J.

The name *Yeshua* rolled along unchanged for centuries, as long as it remained safely ensconced in its familiar Jewish culture. However, as soon as the name got recorded in the Greek of the New Testament, it changed. No one *wanted* to alter the name. It's just that the Greek language has certain limitations that *forced* the name to change.

The New Testament writers wanted to express Hebrew name pronunciations using Greek letters, so that Greek people could read the names from their scrolls and still say the names correctly. The only problem is that the Greek alphabet **has no letter (or even a letter combination) to represent the "sh" sound.** The Greeks of Bible times never even *pronounced* the "sh" sound. (We have no idea how they shushed their kids when they got too rambunctious at the Acropolis.) Whenever the "sh" sounds of foreign words tried to enter their language, the Greeks just replaced all "sh" sounds with the closest sound they had: an "s" sound. This replacement technique sometimes made the Greeks sound like they had a speech impediment. If you could go back in time and ask one of those Greeks to speak or write the English sentence, "She sells seashells by the seashore," he'd end up with "See sells see-sells by the sea-sore."

The second problem with the Greek language is its strict set of **rules which require adding a variety of different suffixes to a noun** (including a proper name like *Yeshua*) **depending on the noun's grammatical function in a sentence**. When a masculine singular noun with a spelling like *Yeshua* is used as the *subject* of a Greek sentence, it must receive a particular suffix. That particular Greek suffix happens to make the name end in an "ooss" sound.[3]

Anyway... here's how the Greeks ended up writing and pronouncing the name *Yeshua*.

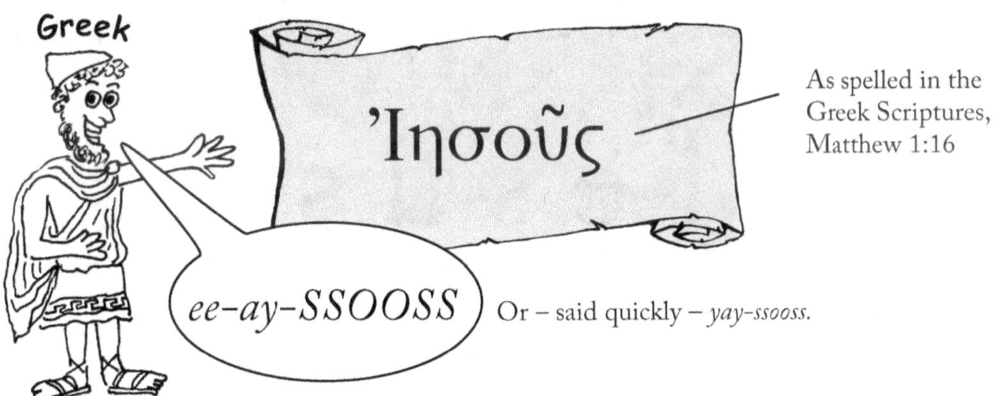

As spelled in the Greek Scriptures, Matthew 1:16

Or – said quickly – *yay-ssooss.*

As you can see, the old Hebrew pronunciation of *yay-SHOO-ah* became slightly altered by the Greek language to *yay-SSOOSS*. We think the New Testament writers made a valiant effort to preserve the original pronunciation, especially given the restrictions they were laboring under. The Greek version is at least close enough to the original name to be *somewhat* recognizable.

---

3. In the Greek language, the *case* of a noun describes its grammatical role in a particular sentence. If a noun is acting as the **subject** of a sentence (as the example in the cartoon scroll above), it is said to be in the **nominative case**. Depending on its case, the name "Jesus" actually receives a variety of different letter endings in the Greek New Testament. There are actually *three different spellings* of the Greek name of Jesus, producing three distinct ending sounds of *ooss, oo,* or *oon*. For example, if Jesus is acting as the recipient of an action (as in "the Spirit descended on Jesus"), then His name receives a suffix which produces an ending sound of *oon*: "*yay-SOON.*" (Unless you're studying Greek, you don't have to worry about memorizing this information. We just wanted you to be aware that the name *Jesus* can and does have three different spellings in Greek.)

Latin was the next language to try its hand at translating the New Testament. Just like Greek, **Latin has no letter or letter combination to represent the "sh" sound**, because Latin doesn't have a "sh" sound. They used the good old Greek trick of replacing the "sh" sound with the Latin sound of "s." And, just like Greek, **Latin adds varying suffixes for its nouns** (including its proper names) **based on the nouns' grammatical functions**, which is why you see the "ooss" sound at the end of the Latin name for *Yeshua* below.

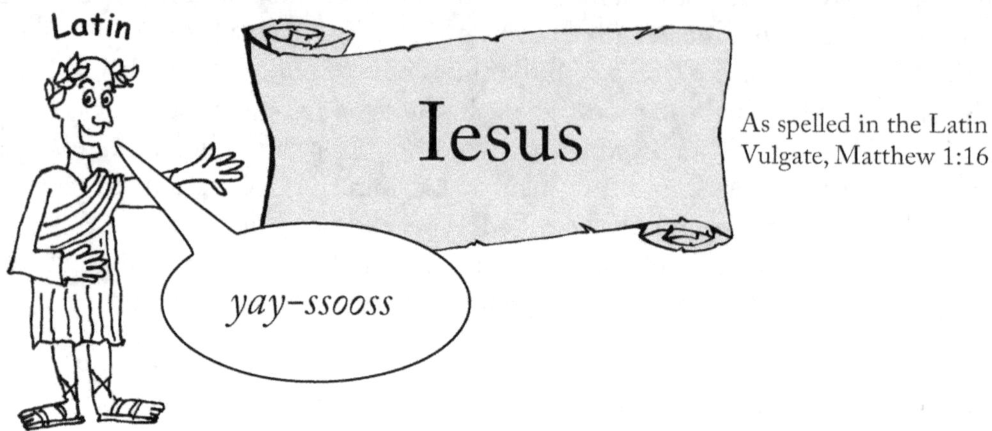

As spelled in the Latin Vulgate, Matthew 1:16

Now, here's a very important point: the Roman alphabet (which Latin uses to write its words) was around centuries before the English language even came into existence. **Classical Latin didn't pronounce its letters the same way the English language pronounces them today, even though the letters look exactly the same.** That's because English *borrowed* the Latin alphabet and altered much of its pronunciation in order to repurpose it for English words. Here's how each letter in the name *Iesus* is actually pronounced in Latin:

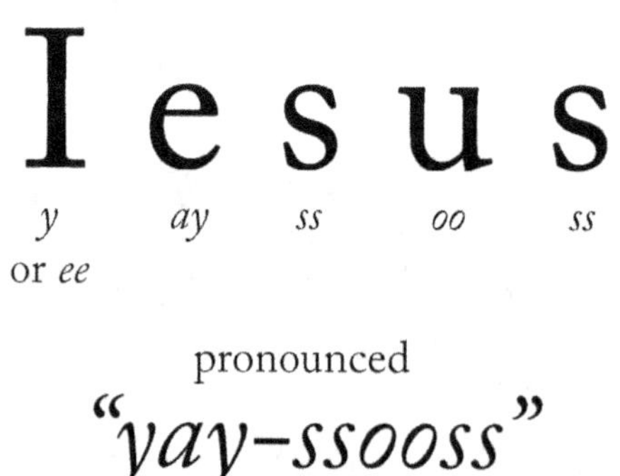

$$\text{I} \quad \text{e} \quad \text{s} \quad \text{u} \quad \text{s}$$

y   ay   ss   oo   ss
or *ee*

pronounced

"yay-ssooss"

Important notes:

The Latin letter *I* or *i* was pronounced like the English *y* or *ee*.

The Latin letter *e* was pronounced either *eh* or *ay*, but never *ee*. In the name *Iesus*, it was pronounced *ay*.

The Latin letter *s* was always pronounced with a soft *s* as in *supple*, never a *z* sound as in *rise*.

The Latin letter *u* was pronounced like the English *oo*.

For many centuries, people the world over would listen to the New Testament being read aloud by their clergy – in Latin – even though in daily life everyone spoke newer languages like Spanish, French, Italian, German and English. Most clergymen read aloud to their flocks from the popular Latin translation called the Latin Vulgate. More time passed, and the people began to request that the Bible be read in their own native languages. This led to the first English translations. Medieval scribes (usually monks) translated and hand copied these first English Bibles. As much as possible, they copied the proper names straight out of the Latin Vulgate, using identical spellings to the ones they saw in Latin. For example, they simple copied the name *Iesus*, as is, directly into their English New Testaments. Over time, these scribes began to introduce a slight change to the shape of the Latin letter *I*. They sometimes added a curl to the bottom of these letters, creating a *J* shape – an alternate form of the letter *I* (called an *allograph*). Now, in English, this *J*-shaped letter came to be pronounced *j* as in *joke*, but not so in Latin. In Latin, the *J*-shaped letter is merely a variant form of the Latin letter *I* and thus is always pronounced *y* or *ee*. The Latin-fluent clergy understood this, of course. They realized that Classical Latin *never* had the sound *j* as in *joke,* since it wasn't until many centuries later that the English language would come along and invent that new sound. So, here's how those clergymen would pronounce the Latin name *Jesus* whenever they read aloud to their congregations:

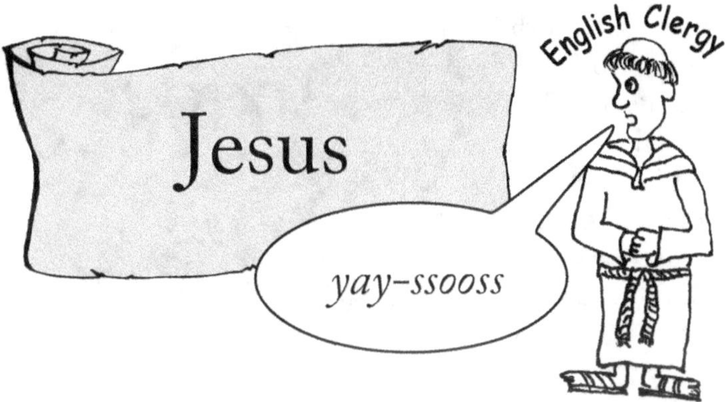

After the Reformation, thousands of lay people began reading their own English Bibles for themselves. Most did not know Latin. They had no idea that the Latin *J* is simply an alternate form of the Latin *I* which sounds like *y*. They didn't realize that the Latin *e* sounds like *ay*, the Latin *s* sounds like *ss* (never *z*), and the Latin *u* sounds like *oo* (not *uh)*. Thus, they came up with many new and bizarre pronunciations of Biblical names, such as the pronunciation *JEE-zuhss.*

Let's Review

Let's review the changes that the name *Yeshua* has undergone throughout the centuries.

1 It all began with the Hebrew name *Y'hoshua* (i.e., "Joshua"), which means "The LORD is salvation."

יְהוֹשֻׁעַ *"y'hō-SHOO-ah"*

2 The later short form of this Hebrew name was *Yeshua*. This form was used by many Jews of Biblical times, including Jesus of Nazareth.

יֵשׁוּעַ *"yay-SHOO-ah"*

3 The Greek New Testament writers transliterated the Hebrew name *Yeshua* as best they could: *ee-ay-ssooss*. Since the Greek language has no "sh" sound and no letters to represent that sound, they went with the closest letter they had – their equivalent to our letter "s." That explains the first "s" sound in his name. But the final "s" sound got added because the Greek language requires that various suffixes be attached to nouns based on the nouns' grammatical roles in sentences.

Ἰησοῦς *"ee-ay-SSOOSS"*

4 The Latin of the Vulgate, like Greek, has no "sh" sound. And, like Greek, Latin must often add an "s" sound to the end of this name because of its own grammatical rules.

Iesus *"yay-ssooss"*

5 English speakers either misunderstood or ignored the intent of their own medieval scribes to pronounce the name using the *Latin* alphabet sounds. Instead, they vocalized the Latin letters using *English* sounds, giving this name an anglicized pronunciation: *JEE-zuhss*. (This pronunciation would have sounded quite bizarre and unrecognizable to anyone alive at the time of Christ.)

Jesus *"jee-zuss"*

Personal Reflections

What was the most surprising or interesting thing that occurred to you as you studied this particular lesson about the Hebrew name יֵשׁוּעַ *Yeshua*?

____

____

____

____

____

____

Knowing that the Hebrew meaning of the name *Jesus* is "The Lord is salvation," record your thoughts about this. List the references for at least two Bible verses that directly connect the name or person of *Jesus* to the concept of *salvation*.

____

____

____

____

____

____

____

____

____

How did our Lord minister His Word directly to your heart through the passages you recorded above? What is He saying to you personally right now through Scripture?

____

____

____

____

____

____

____

When ancient languages act immature

Lesson 2

All the men named *Jesus* in the Old Testament

Joshua Dressed by the Angel, 1886

Then the angel showed me
Joshua the high priest [Yeshua son of Yotsadak]
standing before the angel of the LORD...

Zechariah 3:1

Lesson 2:

All the men named *Jesus* in the Old Testament

Back when we served as leaders of Messianic congregations (places where Jews and Gentiles worship Jesus together), we were often asked challenging questions during oneg[1] which took more than just a few minutes to explain, but we did our best under the time constraints. One frequently asked question came from certain traditional Jewish visitors who would drop in unexpectedly to check us out.

"Wait a minute," they'd say. "What do you mean, the name *Jesus* is Jewish? You mean to tell me there are people named *Jesus* in the TaNaCH?"

"Absolutely," we'd reply. "But the name Jesus has undergone a few changes over the centuries because of Greek, then Latin, then English. Back in Bible times, the name was *Yeshua*."

"Yeah, I get that," they'd frown. "But, I mean, the name *Yeshua* isn't in the TaNaCH, is it? I'm sure I would have heard about that at some point in shul.[2]"

"Not only is the name Yeshua found in the TaNaCH," we'd explain with a smile, "but several different men in the TaNaCH went by that name."

"Well," they'd say, scratching their chins. "Well. I'd sure like to see that."

Here's your chance to see it for yourself. This lesson will list all the places that the name *Yeshua* (usually spelled with the anglicized form *Jeshua* in English translations of the Bible) appears in the Old Testament. We'll present the Scriptures in both Hebrew and English, with the Hebrew name for *Yeshua* highlighted in gray for your convenience.

---

1. **oneg** – a transliteration of the Hebrew word עֹנֶג (pronounced *ō-neg*), meaning *pleasure*. In modern Jewish life, this word has come to be used as shorthand to mean "a festive gathering on the Sabbath, usually involving food, singing, dancing and casual reading of Scripture" – thus fulfilling God's commandment to enjoy the Sabbath.

2. **shul** – a transliteration of the Yiddish word שׁוּל, (pronounced *shool*), meaning *school* or *synagogue*. The word *synagogue* literally just means "meeting," but since the synagogue has traditionally been the place where Jews have always gathered to study Scripture, the word eventually acquired the additional connotation of "school." In modern American Jewish life, the Yiddish term *shul* is now used almost exclusively to refer to the *synagogue* – a congregation and its building – whose purpose is both worship and Bible study.

A few helpful notes before you begin

By the way... if you are completely new to Hebrew but are still feeling adventuresome about taking a glance at the Hebrew phrases below, it will help to know that Hebrew reads from *right* to *left*. Every Hebrew *word* begins at the right and flows leftward, *letter* by *letter*. Likewise, every Hebrew *sentence* begins at the right side of the page and flows leftward, *word* by *word*. Hebrew's unusual directionality will become evident as you attempt to read the italicized definitions we placed underneath each Hebrew word. (However, if you're feeling the least bit uncomfortable about this, please don't feel obligated to even look at the Hebrew phrases.)

Also – and there's no requirement that you actually do this – but if you happen to carefully compare the Hebrew words we highlighted in gray with the standard Hebrew spelling of Yeshua (יֵשׁוּעַ), you might notice the occasional "extra" Hebrew letter attached as a prefix. Such prefixes are just Hebrew prepositions or conjunctions. For example, the Hebrew spelling לְיֵשׁוּעַ means "to Yeshua" or "for Yeshua." In this example, the letter לְ added to the right side (beginning) of His name serves as a prepositional prefix meaning "to" or "for."

Again, it's not required that you pay particular attention to the Hebrew phrases in this lesson. You'll still be able to follow along just fine if you choose to read only the English parts.

Ready to begin? Here are the passages mentioning men named *Yeshua* in the TaNaCH.

The Yeshua who headed the ninth course of the priesthood

הָעֲשִׂרִי.   לִשְׁכַנְיָהוּ   הַתִּשְׁעִי   לְיֵשׁוּעַ

the tenth   *to Sh'chanyahu*   *the ninth*   *to Yeshua*

[7]Now the first lot came forth to Jehoiarib, the second to Jedaiah, [8]the third to Harim, the fourth to Seorim, [9]the fifth to Malchijah, the sixth to Mijamin, [10]the seventh to Hakkoz, the eighth to Abijah, [11]the ninth to **Jeshua**, the tenth to Shecaniah... [19]This was the ordering of them in their service, to come into the house of the Lᴏʀᴅ according to the ordinance [given] to them by Aaron their father, as the Lᴏʀᴅ, the God of Israel, had commanded him (1 Chronicles 24, ᴡᴇʙ[3]).

Context / Commentary

Circa 1010-970 ʙᴄᴇ, King David selected two priests to help create priestly work groups to serve in the Temple. Lots were drawn to designate the order of the priestly courses (or divisions). Each course was named after its head (leader). Every course was in charge of ministering at the temple during its own assigned time period each year. The head of the ninth course was a man named Yeshua.

וְעַל יָדוֹ עֶדֶן, וּמִנְיָמִן, וְיֵשׁוּעַ ...

and by   *his hand*   *Eden*   *and Minyamin*   *and Yeshua*

[11]Then Hezekiah commanded them to prepare rooms in the house of the LORD; and they prepared them. [12]They brought in the offerings and the tithes and the dedicated things faithfully: and over them Conaniah the Levite was ruler, and Shimei his brother was second... [14]Kore the son of Imnah the Levite, the porter at the east [gate], was over the freewill offerings of God, to distribute the offerings of the LORD, and the most holy things. [15]Under him were Eden, and Miniamin, and **Jeshua**, and Shemaiah, Amariah, and Shecaniah, in the cities of the priests, in their office of trust, to give to their brothers by divisions, as well to the great as to the small (2 Chronicles 31, WEB).

Context / Commentary

During King Hezekiah's reign (circa 715-686 BCE), God's temple was cleansed of idols, and the daily and holy day sacrifices were restored. Hezekiah commanded that the people return to bringing their tithes and offerings to provide not only for the burnt offerings of the temple, but also for the portions of the priests and Levites, so that they would be free to give themselves to God's service. A great abundance of contributions were brought, and Hezekiah commanded that storerooms be prepared to hold them all. Certain trusted Levites were then authorized to faithfully distribute these gifts to their fellow priests; Yeshua was one of those trusted men.

---

3. WEB – an abbreviation for "World English Version." Just so you know, throughout this workbook, we did make one change to all of the quotes we've excerpted from this translation of the Bible: we chose to express the unpronounced four-consonant Hebrew name of God with the traditional term "LORD." A little about the World English Version: the WEB is a public-domain translation of the Hebrew Old Testament and Greek New Testament. It's basically an update of the American Standard Version (or ASV, completed in 1901), which at the time was a modernization of the King James Version (or KJV, first written in the 1600s). Our *Messiah's Alphabet* series quotes from a variety of translations – more frequently from those translations in the public domain because of the lack of restrictions on how they may be used. When we have to quote large passages, we tend to lean toward the WEB because it's relatively easy to read and it's in the public domain. However, we're not partial to any one particular version of the Bible. We think that every translation has its pros and cons. We believe that it is advisable and beneficial to consult as many different versions of the Bible as possible when studying Scripture.

Some Yeshuas are hard to tell apart

The two men named Yeshua whom we just presented from the books of first and second Chronicles are pretty easy to distinguish from one another. They lived during different eras – hundreds of years apart – so they couldn't possibly have been the same man. However, we are now going to read about the time period that the Jewish exiles returned from Babylon to Jerusalem, described in the books of Ezra and Nehemiah. Throughout these two books, the name *Yeshua* appears 27 different times, and it is clear from the contexts that these Yeshuas aren't *all* the same man. The question is, though, exactly which of these Yeshua mentions may refer to the same person. Scholars agree there is some overlap, but they don't all agree as to which verses refer to which people. It's difficult to tease them apart due to the lack of detail in some contexts. We'll leave those answers to your own discretion; you might come to an opinion after having had the chance to study the full passages during your personal Bible study time. For the purpose of this workbook, though, we'll be focusing only on the roles these men played in Biblical history.

The Yeshua who helped lead the exiles back to Jerusalem

אֲשֶׁר בָּאוּ עִם זְרֻבָּבֶל, יֵשׁוּעַ, נְחֶמְיָה ...

those [who]   *came*   *with*   *Z'rubavel*   *Yeshua*   *N'chemyah*

¹Now these are the children of the province, who went up out of the captivity of those who had been carried away, whom Nebuchadnezzar the king of Babylon had carried away to Babylon, and who returned to Jerusalem and Judah, everyone to his city; ²who came with Zerubbabel, **Jeshua**, Nehemiah, Seraiah, Reelaiah, Mordecai, Bilshan, Mispar, Bigvai, Rehum, Baanah... (Ezra 2, WEB)

Context / Commentary

Some time following Cyrus' decree in 538 BCE, Zerubbabel and others led all the Jews who wished to return to Israel back with them to Jerusalem. Listed among these leaders in Ezra 2:2 was a man named Yeshua. It is significant that this Yeshua was recorded in the first position in the list of leaders immediately following the name Zerubbabel; clearly this Yeshua was a man of powerful influence and high standing. The Jewish Encyclopedia holds that the Yeshua of this verse was one and the same as the famous Joshua the High Priest (son of Jozadak) who is also mentioned in Ezra chapters 3, 4, 5 and 10, and in Nehemiah chapters 7 and 12. Christian scholars agree with this conclusion. In fact, several Christian translations have gone so far as to replace the name "Jeshua" in Ezra 2:2 with its earlier form, "Joshua," in an attempt to better harmonize it with the form of the name traditionally associated with the historical Joshua the High Priest, thereby hoping to reduce confusion over this man's identity.

עָשָׂר. וּשְׁנַיִם מֵאוֹת שְׁמֹנֶה אַלְפַּיִם יוֹאָב, יֵשׁוּעַ ...לִבְנֵי

[and] ten   *and two*   *hundred*   *eight*   *two thousand*   *[and] Yoav*   *Yeshua*   *of the sons of*

[2]...the number of the men of the people of Israel... [6]The children of Pahathmoab, of the children of **Jeshua** [and] Joab, two thousand eight hundred twelve (Ezra 2, WEB).

הַכֹּהֲנִים – בְּנֵי יְדַעְיָה, לְבֵית יֵשׁוּעַ, תְּשַׁע מֵאוֹת שִׁבְעִים וּשְׁלֹשָׁה.

and three   *seventy*   *hundred*   *nine*   *Yeshua*   *of the house of*   *Y'daiah*   *the sons of*   *the priests*

[36]The priests: the children of Jedaiah, of the house of **Jeshua**, nine hundred seventy-three (Ezra 2, WEB).

הַלְוִיִּם – בְּנֵי יֵשׁוּעַ וְקַדְמִיאֵל, לִבְנֵי הוֹדַוְיָה, שִׁבְעִים וְאַרְבָּעָה.

and four   *seventy*   *Hodavyah*   *of the sons of*   *and Kadmiel*   *Yeshua*   *the sons of*   *the Levites*

[40]The Levites: the children of **Jeshua** and Kadmiel, of the children of Hodaviah, seventy-four (Ezra 2, WEB).

Context / Commentary

The above verses are excerpts from the long list of people who came out of captivity and were led back to Jerusalem by Zerubbabel. Here, we are uncertain if there is any overlap between these three Yeshuas and any others mentioned in the Bible. What can be concluded is that the Yeshuas mentioned here appear to have fathered variant genealogical lines. One line was of lay persons, one was of Levites, and one was specifically of priests.

וַיָּקָם יֵשׁוּעַ בֶּן יוֹצָדָק, וְאֶחָיו הַכֹּהֲנִים ...

and arose	*Yeshua*	*son of*	*Yotsadak*	*and his brothers*	*the priests*

[1]When the seventh month was come, and the children of Israel were in the cities, the people gathered themselves together as one man to Jerusalem. [2]Then stood up **Jeshua** the son of Jozadak, and his brothers the priests, and Zerubbabel the son of Shealtiel, and his brothers, and built the altar of the God of Israel, to offer burnt offerings thereon, as it is written in the law of Moses the man of God. [3]They set the altar on its base; for fear was on them because of the peoples of the countries: and they offered burnt offerings thereon to the LORD, even burnt offerings morning and evening. [4]They kept the feast of tabernacles, as it is written, and [offered] the daily burnt offerings by number, according to the ordinance, as the duty of every day required; [5]and afterward the continual burnt offering, and [the offerings] of the new moons, and of all the set feasts of the LORD that were consecrated, and of everyone who willingly offered a freewill offering to the LORD. [6]From the first day of the seventh month began they to offer burnt offerings to the LORD: but the foundation of the temple of the LORD was not yet laid (Ezra 3, WEB).

Context / Commentary

Once the former exiles had settled back into their homes and the wealthier Jews had made their offerings toward the rebuilding of the temple, all the returnees gathered in Jerusalem in the seventh month. Yeshua the son of Yotsadak (Jeshua the son of Jozadak)[4] rose up and led the effort to rebuild the altar of burnt offerings, even before the temple foundation had been laid. In the face of likely danger from the hostile inhabitants of the land, this was a remarkable act of courage and spiritual leadership. This Yeshua recognized that the highest spiritual priority for the people was reinstituting daily and holy day corporate worship, even above rebuilding the physical edifice of the temple. It was this Yeshua who later became known as that "Joshua the High Priest" who was eulogized in Jewish tradition as one who "builded the house and exalted a people holy to the Lord, prepared for everlasting glory" (Ecclus. [Sirach] xlix.12).[5]

---

4. **Jozadak** (sometimes transliterated *Josedech*) in Hebrew literally means "the LORD is righteous" or "the LORD justifies."

5. This quote is from an extra-Biblical text of ethical teachings called "Ecclesiasticus" (abbreviated "Ecclus." and not to be confused with the Biblical book of Ecclesiastes) recorded by the Jewish scribe Ben Sira (or Sirach) of Jerusalem circa 200-175 BCE. An interesting side note is that this scribe wrote *Ecclesiasticus* under the inspiration of his father, Joshua son of Sirach, who is also widely known among traditional rabbis as *Jesus* son of Sirach or *Yeshua* ben Eliezer ben Sira. It is probable that Sirach was inspired by *both* Yeshuas – his own father, of course, but also the renowned "Yeshua/Joshua the High Priest" of Old Testament times whom he extolled in his book.

... וִישׁוּעַ בֶּן יוֹצָדָק, וּשְׁאָר אֲחֵיהֶם ...

their brothers   and the rest of   Yotsadak   son of   and Yeshua

⁸Now in the second year of their coming to the house of God at Jerusalem, in the second month, began Zerubbabel the son of Shealtiel, and **Jeshua** the son of Jozadak, and the rest of their brothers the priests and the Levites, and all those who were come out of the captivity to Jerusalem, and appointed the Levites, from twenty years old and upward, to have the oversight of the work of the house of the Lord (Ezra 3, web).

וּבָנָיו... קַדְמִיאֵל וְאֶחָיו, בָּנָיו יֵשׁוּעַ וַיַּעֲמֹד

and his sons   Kadmiel   and his brothers   his sons   Yeshua   and arose

⁹Then stood **Jeshua** with his sons and his brothers, Kadmiel and his sons, the sons of Judah, together, to have the oversight of the workmen in the house of God: the sons of Henadad, with their sons and their brothers the Levites (Ezra 3, web).

Context / Commentary

This is the same Yeshua who led the people to rebuild the altar of burnt offerings – Yeshua son of Yotsadak (Jeshua the son of Jozadak) – also known as "Joshua the High Priest." Here, he helps lead the people in the rebuilding of God's temple. The temple is the "house" spoken of by the scribe Sirach in his book of ethics, where he says that this Yeshua was the one who "builded the house and exalted a people holy to the Lord, prepared for everlasting glory" (see footnote, previous page).

וַיֹּאמֶר לָהֶם זְרֻבָּבֶל, וְיֵשׁוּעַ, וּשְׁאָר רָאשֵׁי הָאָבוֹת לְיִשְׂרָאֵל...

| and said | to them | Z'rubavel | and Yeshua | and the rest of | the heads of | the fathers | of Israel |

¹Now when the adversaries of Judah and Benjamin heard that the children of the captivity were building a temple to the Lord, the God of Israel; ²then they drew near to Zerubbabel, and to the heads of fathers' [houses], and said to them, "Let us build with you; for we seek your God, as you do; and we sacrifice to him since the days of Esar Haddon king of Assyria, who brought us up here." ³But Zerubbabel, and **Jeshua**, and the rest of the heads of fathers' [houses] of Israel, said to them, "You have nothing to do with us in building a house to our God; but we ourselves together will build to the Lord, the God of Israel, as king Cyrus the king of Persia has commanded us."

⁴Then the people of the land weakened the hands of the people of Judah, and troubled them in building, ⁵and hired counselors against them, to frustrate their purpose, all the days of Cyrus king of Persia, even until the reign of Darius king of Persia (Ezra 4, web).

Context / Commentary

This Yeshua — along with the rest of the chief fathers of Israel — stood like a wall against the adversaries in the land who sought to hinder the work of rebuilding God's temple. We may safely assume this Yeshua to be Jeshua son of Jozadak, or Joshua the High Priest, since his name is listed here immediately following Zerubbabel's in its usual position indicating high authority. The situation also fits with the overall context of the role of Jeshua son of Jozadak at that time: the Yeshua who was actively leading the rebuilding efforts.

... יֵשׁוּעַ   בֶּן   יוֹזָבָד   וְעִמָּהֶם   פִּינְחָס   בֶּן   אֶלְעָזָר   וְעִמּוֹ ...

Yeshua   *son of*   *Yozavad*   *and with them*   *Pinchas*   *son of*   *El'azar*   *and with him*

[33]On the fourth day the silver and the gold and the vessels were weighed in the house of our God into the hand of Meremoth the son of Uriah the priest; and with him was Eleazar the son of Phinehas; and with them was Jozabad the son of **Jeshua**, and Noadiah the son of Binnui, the Levite; [34]the whole by number and by weight: and all the weight was written at that time (Ezra 8, WEB).

Context / Commentary

Jozabad was the son of a man named Yeshua. Jozabad was entrusted – along with several others – with the solemn role of overseeing the thorough accounting of the weight of the silver, gold and vessels of the house of God. It is unclear which Yeshua was the father of Jozabad, but, considering the high level of trustworthiness and accountability required for this job, it would not be unreasonable to guess that Jozabad's father may have been that Yeshua known as Joshua the High Priest.

The Yeshua whose relatives disobediently married foreign wives

...אֲשֶׁר   הֹשִׁיבוּ   נָשִׁים   נָכְרִיּוֹת   מִבְּנֵי   יֵשׁוּעַ   בֶּן   יוֹצָדָק,   וְאֶחָיו...

and his brothers   *Yotsadak*   *son of*   *Yeshua*   *of the sons of*   *pagan*   *wives*   *had taken*   *who*

[18]Among the sons of the priests there were found who had married foreign women: [namely], of the sons of **Jeshua**, the son of Jozadak, and his brothers, Maaseiah, and Eliezer, and Jarib, and Gedaliah. [19]They gave their hand that they would put away their wives; and being guilty, [they offered] a ram of the flock for their guilt (Ezra 10, WEB).

Context / Commentary

Four descendants of Yeshua son of Jozadak and his brothers were guilty of having married foreign wives in disobedience to God's commandment. After a period of corporate mourning and repentance, these four men and all the others guilty of this sin divorced these women. These four descendants of Yeshua, being priests, also offered a ram for their trespass.

... יֵשׁוּעַ   בֶּן   עֶזֶר   יָדוֹ   עַל   וַיְחַזֵּק

Yeshua   *son of*   *Ezer*   *his hand*   *at*   *and repaired*

[19]Next to him repaired Ezer the son of **Jeshua**, the ruler of Mizpah, another portion, over against the ascent to the armory at the turning [of the wall]. [20]After him Baruch the son of Zabbai earnestly repaired another portion, from the turning [of the wall] to the door of the house of Eliashib the high priest (Nehemiah 3, WEB).

Context / Commentary

The book of Nehemiah describes how the exiles from Babylon returned to Israel and rebuilt the wall and gates surrounding Jerusalem, which had been reduced to rubble in their absence. In this chapter, Nehemiah describes in detail which builders repaired which parts of the wall. It is unclear if the Yeshua who fathered the Ezer who repaired this section of the wall is the same man as any other Yeshuas mentioned in Scripture.

The Yeshuas who were the fathers of clans in Israel (repeated)

Ezra and Nehemiah were leaders who worked together on restoring Jerusalem after the exile. Like the book of Ezra, the book of Nehemiah also includes a genealogical list of the people who came back from the Babylonian captivity. Much of this list is similar to that of Ezra. You've already studied those names of Yeshua in detail in this lesson.

Rather than repeat those listings here, we encourage you to complete a very quick and simple exercise as a kind of review. Read through Nehemiah chapter 7 in any English translation, looking for mentions of those Joshuas or Jeshuas you've already learned about in the book of Ezra. Hint: you'll find them all in the following verses:

7:7   "Who came with Zerubbabel, **Jeshua**, Nehemiah, Azariah..."

7:11   "...of the children of **Jeshua** and Joab..."

7:39   "...the children of Jedaiah, of the house of **Jeshua**..."

7:43   "...the children of **Jeshua**, of Kadmiel..."

יָמִין...   וְשֵׁרֵבְיָה,   וּבָנִי,   וְיֵשׁוּעַ,

Yamin   *and Sherevyah*   *and Bani*   *and Yeshua*

⁵Ezra opened the book in the sight of all the people; (for he was above all the people;) and when he opened it, all the people stood up: ⁶and Ezra blessed the Lᴏʀᴅ, the great God. All the people answered, "Amen, Amen," with the lifting up of their hands. They bowed their heads, and worshiped the Lᴏʀᴅ with their faces to the ground. ⁷Also **Jeshua**, and Bani, and Sherebiah, Jamin, Akkub, Shabbethai, Hodiah, Maaseiah, Kelita, Azariah, Jozabad, Hanan, Pelaiah, and the Levites, caused the people to understand the law: and the people [stood] in their place. ⁸They read in the book, in the law of God, distinctly; and they gave the sense, so that they understood the reading (Nehemiah 8, ᴡᴇʙ).

Context / Commentary

In this passage – one of the most touching and beautiful in all of Scripture – Ezra reads from the Torah scroll in the hearing of all the congregated returnees. Most of these listeners had long neglected the Word of God. As Ezra read aloud, a man named Yeshua, along with many others, plainly explained Scripture's meaning. The listeners then wept under the moving conviction of the Holy Spirit.

Ezra reads the Law. Trial proof of a book illustration by Dutch engraver Pieter Mortier for an illustrated print Bible published in 1700. (Rijksmuseum, Amsterdam.)

... כִּי לֹא עָשׂוּ מִימֵי יֵשׁוּעַ בֶּן נוּן ...

for	not	had done	from the days of	Yeshua	son of	Nun

[13]On the second day were gathered together the heads of fathers' [houses] of all the people, the priests, and the Levites, to Ezra the scribe, even to give attention to the words of the law. [14]They found written in the law how that the LORD had commanded by Moses that the children of Israel should dwell in booths in the feast of the seventh month... [17]All the assembly of those who were come again out of the captivity made booths and lived in the booths; for since the days of **Jeshua** the son of Nun to that day the children of Israel had not done so. There was very great gladness (Nehemiah 8, WEB).

Context / Commentary

The day after Ezra's reading of the Law (described on the previous page), the leaders of Israel assembled to read some more. They found the portion describing the Feast of Tabernacles, so they instructed the people to celebrate it. Nehemiah 8:17 pointedly makes mention of Joshua son of Nun (Moses' successor and the man who led Israel in their conquest of the promised land), but uses the late-form spelling of the name, which is Yeshua. Nehemiah here was drawing a spiritual connection between the era of Joshua son of Nun (a long and difficult campaign to initially possess the land), and Nehemiah's own era (a long and difficult campaign to possess the land all over again). Part of the great symbolism of the Feast of Tabernacles is God's promise that His people will one day dwell in peace in their own land under the spiritual Tabernacle of God's glory. Yeshua son of Nun is a spiritual symbol of Messiah Yeshua, who leads believers into a "promised land" of spiritual peaceful rest today, and will also bring about a future thousand-year period of physical peace on earth.

וַיָּקָם עַל מַעֲלֵה הַלְוִיִּם יֵשׁוּעַ, וּבָנִי, ...

and stood — upon — the stairs of — the Levites — Yeshua — and Bani

וַיֹּאמְרוּ הַלְוִיִּם, יֵשׁוּעַ, וְקַדְמִיאֵל, בָּנִי ...

and said — the Levites — Yeshua — and Kadmiel — Bani

וְהַלְוִיִּם – וְיֵשׁוּעַ בֶּן אֲזַנְיָה ...

and the Levites — and Yeshua — son of — Azanyah

⁴Then stood up on the stairs of the Levites, **Jeshua**, and Bani, Kadmiel, Shebaniah, Bunni, Sherebiah, Bani, [and] Chenani, and cried with a loud voice to the LORD their God. ⁵Then the Levites, **Jeshua**, and Kadmiel, Bani, Hashabneiah, Sherebiah, Hodiah, Shebaniah, [and] Pethahiah, said, "Stand up and bless the LORD your God from everlasting to everlasting! Blessed be your glorious name, which is exalted above all blessing and praise! ... ³⁸Yet for all this, we make a sure covenant, and write it; and our princes, our Levites, [and] our priests, seal to it" (Nehemiah 9, WEB).

¹Now those who sealed were: Nehemiah the governor, the son of Hacaliah, and Zedekiah... ⁸Maaziah, Bilgai, Shemaiah; these were the priests. ⁹The Levites: namely, **Jeshua** the son of Azaniah, Binnui of the sons of Henadad, Kadmiel... (Nehemiah 10, WEB).

Context / Commentary

After Ezra's momentous reading of the Law and upon concluding the celebration of the Feast of Tabernacles, all the sons of Israel assembled for a corporate fast, confessing their sins. On the twenty-fourth day of the seventh month, they spent a quarter of the day reading the Torah, then another quarter confessing and worshiping. The civil and spiritual leaders of Israel – among them a certain Levite named Yeshua (son of Azaniah) – stood before all the people and cried out with a loud voice to God. He joined with the other spiritual leaders in a formal speech which blessed God, recited their long history as His people, confessed their stubborn disobedience over all those years, and requested His mercy once again. At the conclusion of this speech, they formally renewed the covenant in writing on behalf of all the people, signing it and giving it their official seal.

פֶּלֶט ... וּבְבֵית, וּבְמוֹלָדָה, וּבִישׁוּעַ

Pelet	*and in Beth*	*and in Moladah*	*and in Yeshua*

[25]As for the villages, with their fields, some of the children of Judah lived in Kiriath Arba and its towns, and in Dibon and its towns, and in Jekabzeel and its villages, [26]and in **Jeshua**, and in Moladah, and Beth Pelet, [27]and in Hazar Shual, and in Beersheba and its towns... (Nehemiah 11, WEB)

Context / Commentary

Nehemiah chapter 11 contains a list of where the rulers, priests and Levites settled. Verse 26 refers to a village called Yeshua, probably so named for the ancestral name of the clan that inhabited it.

For the people of the 1500s, Joshua the High Priest was a famous figure. This portrait is of Joshua the High Priest as imagined by Guillaume Rouille in his 1553 iconography book containing 950 fine woodcut portraits in medallion form, *Promptuarii Iconum insigniorum a Seculo Hominum* ("Repository of Portraits of Notable Men of the World"). Surrounding this portrait of Joshua are the Latin words *SUM SACER IEHOSUA* – "I am Y'hoshua the Priest." The Latin transliteration *Iehosua* of the Hebrew name יְהוֹשֻׁעַ *Y'hoshua* is Latin's best approximation; the Latin language has no such sound as "sh," so a simple *S* had to be substituted.

Nehemiah chapter 12 lists the priestly and Levitical leaders during the different High Priestly successions: Yeshua son of Yotsadak (Joshua the High Priest), then his son, Joiakim – the high priest who succeeded him – and the generations which followed: Eliashib, then Joiada, then Jonathan (Johanan), then Jaddua. Throughout this chapter, different men named Yeshua are mentioned. You've already read their names multiple times in the books of Ezra and Nehemiah as you studied this lesson; in Nehemiah 12, they are repeated. For your convenience, we have categorized the verses in chapter 12 by each individual man.

Mentions of Yeshua son of Yotsadak (Jeshua son of Jozadak, or "Joshua the High Priest")

12:1   "Now these are the priests and the Levites who went up with Zerubbabel the son of Shealtiel, and **Jeshua**..."

12:7   "...These were the chiefs of the priests and of their brothers in the days of **Jeshua**."

12:10   "**Jeshua** became the father of Joiakim, and Joiakim became the father of Eliashib, and Eliashib became the father of Joiada..."

12:26   "These were in the days of Joiakim the son of **Jeshua**, the son of Jozadak, and in the days of Nehemiah the governor, and of Ezra the priest the scribe."

Mention of Yeshua, a leader of the Levites, during the days of Joshua the High Priest

12:8   "Moreover the Levites: **Jeshua**, Binnui, Kadmiel..."

Mention of Yeshua son of Kadmiel, a leader of the Levites, during the days of Eliashib, Joiada, Johanan and Jaddua

12:24   "The chiefs of the Levites: Hashabiah, Sherebiah, and **Jeshua** the son of Kadmiel..."

וְאֶל יְהוֹשֻׁעַ בֶּן יְהוֹצָדָק, הַכֹּהֵן הַגָּדוֹל ...

| and to | Y'hoshua | son of | Y'hotsadak | the priest | high |

¹In the second year of Darius the king, in the sixth month, in the first day of the month, the Word of the Lord came by Haggai, the prophet, to Zerubbabel, the son of Shealtiel, governor of Judah, and to **Joshua**, the son of Jehozadak, the high priest, saying, ²"This is what the Lord of Armies says: These people say, 'The time hasn't yet come, the time for the Lord's house to be built.'" ³Then the Word of the Lord came by Haggai, the prophet, saying, ⁴"Is it a time for you yourselves to dwell in your paneled houses, while this house lies waste? ⁵Now therefore this is what the Lord of Armies says: Consider your ways..." (Haggai 1, WEB)

Context / Commentary

Back in Ezra 5, there was a brief mention of the fact that the Lord spoke through Haggai the prophet to stir up the people to rebuild the Lord's house. Here, in the book of Haggai, the exact words of this prophecy have been recorded in detail for our benefit. By the time of Haggai chapter 1, the people had obtained more than adequate shelter for their immediate families; in fact, they were living comfortably in what God called "paneled" or "wainscoted" houses. God was warning the people of their self-serving focus and calling them to return their priorities to spiritual things. He wanted them to stop neglecting their relationship with Him.

Note that this reference is unique among all others in this lesson. This is the first time that we selected a Scripture passage that does not include the specific spelling of "Yeshua." Instead, it uses "Y'hoshua" (Joshua). There's a good reason we thought you needed to see this particular verse, though. The full context of Haggai chapter 1 makes it abundantly clear that the one whom Haggai called "Joshua son of Josedech" is one and the same person as that famous Yeshua son of Yotsadak known as "Joshua the High Priest" – the man you've studied so much already, who played such a pivotal role in the books of Ezra and Nehemiah. Yet, in those books, Scripture chose to record that man's name as "Yeshua" (Jeshua), not Joshua. Why? Because the names are really the same, just as "Rob" or "Bob" are really the same as "Robert."

We included this reference to drive home the point that the names Yeshua/Jeshua and Y'hoshua/Joshua are interchangeable in Scripture. Yeshua/Jeshua is simply a shortened, alternate form of Y'hoshua/Joshua.

The Yeshuas of the Old Testament are symbolic types of Messiah Yeshua

If you believe in Yeshua of Nazareth as Savior and LORD, you might have noticed some of the symbolic "types" or "shadows" of Him that were portrayed by the roles of these men named Yeshua in the TaNaCH. (If you didn't happen to notice any symbolic types at all, that's perfectly normal, by the way. Remember: you've had to absorb an absolute *flood* of new information in this lesson. While you were focused on learning all about those Old Testament Yeshuas, you had little attention to spare for anything else.) So now, for your convenience, we've compiled a brief list of the roles played by those Old Testament Yeshuas. Take a moment to think about all the roles our Messiah Yeshua fulfills, then compare them to those in the list below.

The Old Testament Yeshua who...

- was a leader of the priesthood

- distributed holy offerings to his fellow priests

- helped lead the exiles back to Jerusalem

- led the rebuilding of God's altar of burnt offerings

- helped lead the rebuilding of the temple

- stood against the adversaries of Israel

- had a son that helped record the temple treasure

- had sons that disobediently married foreign wives

- had a son that helped rebuild Jerusalem's wall

- explained God's Torah to the people

- symbolized possession of the Promised Land

- helped mediate and seal a renewed covenant

- had a village named after him

- was a high priest

We noticed many ways in which our Messiah Yeshua's life and ministry is foreshadowed by the Yeshuas of the Old Testament. Here's what we came up with; perhaps you'll think of others.

Old Testament (TaNaCH) Symbolic Types in the Historical Men Named Yeshua	New Testament (B'rit Chadashah) Fulfillments in Yeshua of Nazareth
Yeshuas who were leaders of the priesthood	"You also, as living stones, are built up as a spiritual house, to be a holy priesthood, to offer up spiritual sacrifices, acceptable to God through Jesus Christ" (1 Peter 2:5).
A Yeshua who served as high priest over all Israel	"Having then a great high priest, who has passed through the heavens, Jesus [Yeshua], the Son of God, let us hold tightly to our confession" (Hebrews 4:14).
A Yeshua who distributed holy offerings from an abundant temple treasury to his fellow priests	"that he would grant you, according to the riches of his glory, that you may be strengthened with power through his Spirit in the inward man" (Ephesians 3:16).
A Yeshua who had a son who was entrusted with stewardship of the temple treasury	"So let a man think of us as Christ's servants, and stewards of God's mysteries. Here, moreover, it is required of stewards that they be found faithful" (1 Corinthians 4:1-2).
A Yeshua who helped lead the formerly captive exiles back to a life of freedom	"The Spirit of the Lord is on me, because he has anointed me to preach good news to the poor. He has sent me to heal the brokenhearted, to proclaim release to the captives, recovering of sight to the blind, to deliver those who are crushed, and to proclaim the acceptable year of the Lord" (the words of Yeshua, Luke 4:18-19).

              Lesson 2: All the men named *Jesus* in the Old Testament

Old Testament (TaNaCH) Symbolic Types in the Historical Men Named Yeshua	New Testament (B'rit Chadashah) Fulfillments in Yeshua of Nazareth
A Yeshua who symbolized possession of the promised land – a place of peaceful rest for God's people	"Let us fear therefore, lest perhaps anyone of you should seem to have come short of a promise of entering into his rest. For we who have believed do enter into that rest... For if Joshua had given them rest, he would not have spoken afterward of another day. There remains therefore a Sabbath rest for the people of God" (Hebrews 4:1,3,8-9)
A Yeshua who stood against the adversaries of Israel	"He went into their synagogues throughout all Galilee, preaching and casting out demons" (Mark 1:39). "I heard a loud voice in heaven, saying, 'Now is come the salvation, the power, and the Kingdom of our God, and the authority of his Christ; for the accuser of our brothers has been thrown down, who accuses them before our God day and night'" (Revelation 12:10).
A Yeshua who was high priest and who led the rebuilding of God's altar of burnt offerings and the rebuilding of the temple	"...We have such a high priest, who sat down on the right hand of the throne of the Majesty in the heavens, a servant of the sanctuary, and of the true tabernacle, which the Lord pitched, not man" (Hebrews 8:1-2).
A Yeshua who had disobedient sons and relatives that later repented, found grace, and remained within the family of Israel	"The son said to him, 'Father, I have sinned against heaven, and in your sight. I am no longer worthy to be called your son.' But the father said to his servants, 'Bring out the best robe, and put it on him. Put a ring on his hand, and shoes on his feet. Bring the fattened calf, kill it, and let us eat, and celebrate; for this, my son, was dead, and is alive again. He was lost, and is found.' They began to celebrate" (a parable of Yeshua, Luke 15: 21-24) "For I will be merciful to their unrighteousness. I will remember their sins and lawless deeds no more" (God's future promise to Israel, Hebrews 8:12).

Old Testament (TaNaCH) Symbolic Types in the Historical Men Named Yeshua	New Testament (B'rit Chadashah) Fulfillments in Yeshua of Nazareth
A Yeshua who had a son who helped rebuild Jerusalem's wall	"According to the grace of God which was given to me, as a wise master builder I laid a foundation, and another builds on it. But let each man be careful how he builds on it. For no one can lay any other foundation than that which has been laid, which is Jesus Christ" (the words of Rav Shaul/Rabbi Paul, 1 Corinthians 3:10-11).
A Yeshua who explained God's Torah to the people	"Beginning from Moses and from all the prophets, [Yeshua] explained to them in all the Scriptures the things concerning himself... They said one to another, 'Weren't our hearts burning within us while he spoke to us along the way, and while he opened the Scriptures to us?'" (Luke 24:27,32)
A Yeshua who helped mediate, write and seal a renewed covenant on behalf of the people	"But now he has obtained a more excellent ministry, by so much as he is also the mediator of a better covenant, which on better promises has been given as law... 'For this is the covenant that I will make with the house of Israel. After those days,' says the Lord, 'I will put my laws into their mind, I will also write them on their heart. I will be their God, and they will be my people'" (Hebrews 8:6,10). "Now he who establishes us with you in Christ, and anointed us, is God, who also sealed us, and gave us the down payment of the Spirit in our hearts" (2 Corinthians 1:21-22).
A Yeshua who had a village named after him, where his sons and their later generations dwelled	"I saw the holy city, New Jerusalem, coming down out of heaven from God, prepared like a bride adorned for her husband... There will in no way enter into it anything profane, or one who causes an abomination or a lie, but only those who are written in the Lamb's book of life" (Revelation 21:2,27).

Personal Reflections

What was the most surprising or interesting thing that occurred to you as you studied this particular lesson about יֵשׁוּעַ *Yeshua*?

____

____

____

____

____

____

How did our LORD minister His Word directly to your heart through the passages in this lesson? What is He saying to you personally right now through Scripture?

____

____

____

____

____

____

____

For additional meditation on the wonderful and powerful name of Yeshua, here's a great exercise. Go back through the list of New Testament fulfillments on the previous three pages. Find at least one other New Testament reference that speaks about each fulfillment and record your new-found references on a piece of notebook paper. (Hint: Bible software, Bible apps or searchable Scripture websites can automate and streamline your search for particular words and phrases throughout the New Testament. We urge you to make use of these tools if you have access to them.)

If you are participating in a class or small group that is completing this workbook together, go around the room and read the verses you found to one another. Prepare to be amazed by what the Holy Spirit reveals you all share your findings!

Lesson 3

"Core" Meanings

"And so I think we have no choice but to conclude that the meaning of opaque is unclear."
SYMPOSIUM OF DICTIONARY WRITERS

Lesson 3:

"Core" meanings

We'd like to start this lesson with a little story.

Once upon a time, a very nice lady named Jane wanted to write a dictionary. She invited several of her friends to help. She was careful to invite people from a wide range of experience, each working in a different industry or area of expertise. They all sat around a big table while Jane stood at a large whiteboard to write down their ideas.

"Everyone, I'm having a little trouble with the definition of the word *branch*," Jane said. "I'd like to just go around the room and get your thoughts on how to define it." She gave everyone a moment to think in silence.

After a pause, the biologist spoke up. "A branch is the arm of a tree, deviating from the main trunk, from which leaves, flowers or fruits grow."

Jane wrote this definition on the board.

The bank president cleared his throat. "Actually, I was thinking more along the lines of a division of a company, like one of our bank's branches."

Jane kept writing, adding this definition to the whiteboard.

"What about the tributary of a river?" asked the geologist. "That certainly qualifies as a branch."

"Or a fork in a roadway," said the civil engineer, who was nodding in approval at the geologist's answer. "It's where the road makes a branch, just like a river."

"You know what I was thinking?" said the lawyer. "I was thinking about the branches of government, like judicial, executive, legislative, etc."

"Me too," said the policeman. "Except my mind went straight to the branches of the military."

"What about a specific division of a family tree?" suggested the genealogist.

"Or a branch of the sewer?" added the plumber.

"Here's one," said the computer programmer. "A branch is a set of instructions in a computer program that tells the machine to deviate from its default behavior."

Jane finally finished writing and turned away from the whiteboard to face the group again. Chuckling, she made a T shape with her hands to signal a timeout. "Okay, those are all really great suggestions. And, even though they're all different from each other, they're all accurate. Now you can see why I needed your help. Can anyone suggest *one single definition* that describes the *core meaning* of the word 'branch'? I'm really looking for the *essence* of the word. Let's see if we can come up with a definition that encompasses all the ideas we just listed."

"How about this?" offered the linguist. "How about... *Branch: a division extending from the central structure.*"

Silence fell as everyone mentally tested this core meaning to see if it fit his or her own suggestion. Soon, everyone was nodding and smiling.

"Yep, it works for me!" said one.

"Me, too!" said another.

"Perfect!" said Jane. "I think our linguist's core definition describes every definition listed on the whiteboard. Let's take a break. Coffee and donuts for everyone!"

Core meanings result in rich and varied translations

The little story on the previous page illustrates the variety of meanings that any word can have, all depending on its context. You can see how the core meaning of the word "branch" can be applied across many different situations to arrive at new meanings which are very specific to the context in which it appears. It's crucial to remember that a word's **application** (*how it is applied and in what context*) strongly affects the word's **meaning** in that context.

The same thing is true of **all words in all languages**. In the Hebrew of the Scriptures, we especially see this principle of **flexibility in translation**. This means that **the core meaning of a word can express itself in varying definitions which are specific to the context.** (This is the reason that Bible translators have such a tough job. Languages are not like machine codes in which a term from one language may *always* be used to represent a term from another language.)

Understanding this, then, it's time to learn the core meaning of the name יֵשׁוּעַ *Yeshua*.

The core meaning of the Hebrew name *Yeshua*

Let's begin to learn about the **core meaning** of the Hebrew name יֵשׁוּעַ *Yeshua*. *Yeshua* is just a short form of יְהוֹשֻׁעַ *Y'hoshua*, which itself is a contraction of two different Hebrew words.

The first Hebrew word in *Y'hoshua* is an abbreviated form of the holy, personal name of God, יהוה. It's the part of the name *Y'hoshua* that sounds like *Y'ho–*. This is why we know that "Joshua" actually means "the Lord is salvation" rather than merely "salvation" – we are able to clearly see and hear that old, familiar *Y'ho–* prefix for the personal name of God that appears in so many Hebrew names of Biblical people.

The second Hebrew word in *Y'hoshua* finds its roots in the verb יָשַׁע *yasha*, whose core meaning is *to make (or to be made) open, wide or free*. This verbal root has a variety of applications which, depending on context, can mean *safety, deliverance, rescue, preservation, defense* or *victory*. Picture a man who is confined – trapped – closed in by his troubles, or completely surrounded by danger. If he is somehow removed from that situation, he finds himself in a *wide open place* (physically or figuratively) where he is then *free* of his former difficult circumstances.

You can imagine all the possible meanings that can arise from this core meaning of *wide open freedom*, depending on the context. The *Brown-Driver-Briggs Lexicon* (BDB) provides the following translations of יָשַׁע *yasha*:

- to give width and breadth to, to liberate, to deliver (from physical or moral troubles)
- to be placed in freedom, to be liberated (as above)
- to save (or be saved) in battle, to be victorious, to be in a place of safety

The BDB also comments that Arabic – a sister language to Hebrew – has its own version of this verb, meaning *to be capacious, to make wide or spacious, to make sufficient*, or *to live in abundance*. All these varied meanings apply to the life and ministry of Yeshua, who "saves us" (Hebrews 7:25), gives us life "more abundantly" (John 10:10) and "sets us free" (John 8:36).

Following is a list (not exhaustive) of some applications of the verb **ע.שׁ.ע** *yasha* in various contexts of the Hebrew scriptures.

How the Hebrew verb *yasha* is translated	Scripture reference and Bible version which uses this translation	How this translation is related to the core meaning of *wide open freedom* in its particular context
"saved"	Exodus 14:30, KJV	*freed* from physical attack
"delivered"	Judges 3:9, DRB	*freed* from physical servitude
"free"	Judges 10:1, GNT	*freed* from fear of enemies
"defend"	Judges 10:1, KJV	*freed* from fear of enemies
"avenging"	1 Samuel 25:26, KJV	*freed* from a debt of honor
"preserved"	2 Samuel 8:6, KJV	territorial/financial *freedom*
"help"	2 Samuel 10:19, NIV	*freed* from retaliation
"victory"	Psalm 98:1, NAS	*freed* from unrighteousness
"rescue"	Zechariah 8:13, NLT	*freed* from accursedness
"deliver"	Ezekiel 37:23, KJV	*freed* from sinful backsliding

Recognizing Hebrew words by their roots

Core meanings are usually stored and propagated in the form of **roots**. An example of a root in English is the four-letter spelling *dict*. From this root's core meaning of "to say," we get words like *dictation* ("*saying* words out loud"), *benediction* ("a good *saying*," i.e., "blessing") and *predict* ("to *say* in advance"). You can tell that these three words all share the same core meaning, because they all share the same root, *dict*. If you're actively searching for the root *dict* in a list of words, it's not hard to find. In fact, the root becomes fairly obvious if you're able to train yourself to ignore the prefixes and suffixes surrounding it.

Similarly, **Hebrew words have roots** – certain letters shared in common with other Hebrew words which you can learn to recognize with practice. Whenever you see the **same two or three consonant Hebrew letters in the same order**, and whenever they are **not** a prefix or a suffix, then you'll know that these letters are **root letters**; that's where the core meaning is stored.

The Hebrew spellings of *Yeshua* and *Y'hoshua*

Let's take a closer look at the Hebrew name  *Yeshua*. Here it is, nice and large:

And here's the older, alternate form of His name: יְהוֹשֻׁעַ *Y'hoshua*. Again, nice and large:

First, we're going to concentrate on the older name *Y'hoshua*. If you've completed Book 1 of our Hebrew language series, then you already know the names of these letters and how they sound. If you haven't had the chance to learn the Hebrew alphabet yet, we've included a graphic on the next page which describes each letter and sound in detail for you.

    Lesson 3: "Core" meanings

Take a look at the following enlarged graphic. We've written the letter name and how it sounds next to each letter. Remember that **Hebrew is read from right to left,** so you must begin at the **right** side of the word, where the arrow is.

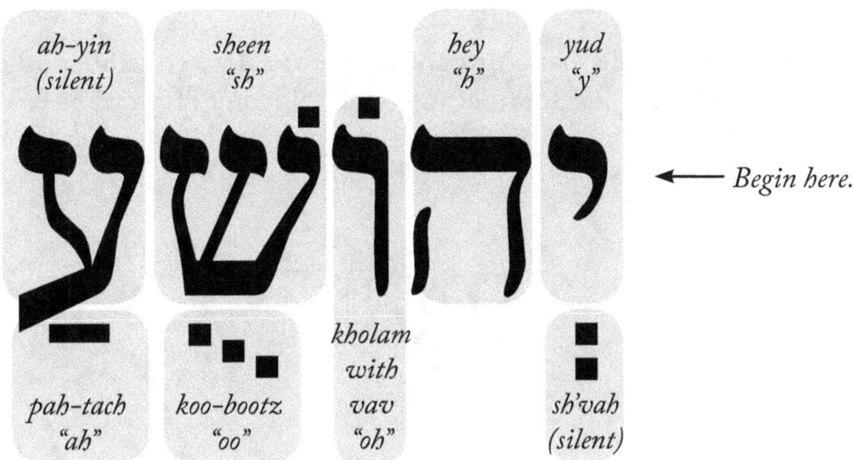

In order, from **right to left**, we have the following consonants and vowels:

׳	*yud*	"y"	consonant
׃	*sh'vah*	(silent)	vowel
ה	*hey*	"h"	consonant
ו	*kholam with vav*	"oh"	vowel
שׁ	*sheen*	"sh"	consonant
	koo-bootz	"oo"	vowel
ע	*ah-yin*	(silent)	consonant
־	*pah-tach*	"ah"	vowel

Putting it all together smoothly, we end up with the pronunciation *Y'hoshua*.

Now we'll split the name in half to illustrate that the first half (right half) of the name comes from an abbreviated form of the personal name of God, and the second half (left half) comes from the root letters of the verb *yasha – to free, to deliver, to save.*

Complete meaning: "The LORD is salvation."

Recognizing the Hebrew root letters from the verb *yasha* in the names *Y'hoshua* and *Yeshua*

Now, in Hebrew, there's a rule that **only consonants are allowed to be root letters**. Ignoring the first half of the name *Y'hoshua* below (because that half comes from the personal name of God), let's focus on just the *second* half. To illustrate, we've colored in the root letters that originate from the verb *yasha, to save.*

Let's take our new knowledge of these root letters and examine the name *Yeshua* now. If you've ever studied Hebrew, you'll be able to differentiate the vowels from the consonants in this name. If you haven't, that's no problem. We placed gray boxes around the consonants for you:

Recall that the name *Yeshua* is just an abbreviated form of *Y'hoshua*, so that means the first letter (at the far right) comes from the personal name of God. We'll ignore that letter for now. The remainder of the name *Yeshua* comes from the root letters of the verb *yasha, to save*. Since only consonants can count as root letters, we'll ignore the vowels in that part of the name, too. Here is our illustration showing only the root letters from *yasha* colored in:

Comparing the two, we now can clearly see the root *yasha, to save,* in both names:

Y'hoshua (Joshua)

Yeshua (Jeshua or *Jesus)*

The root letters of *yasha* may form a variety of verbs, nouns and adjectives

One of the most eye-opening exercises you can do to better understand the Word of God is trace a word's *root* throughout Scripture. By this, we mean tracing all the various words that could made using the same root letters – be they verbs, nouns or adjectives. (Today's computer programs, websites and apps make this task easier than ever.) For example, we could begin by studying all the **verbal spellings** in Scripture that use the Hebrew root ע.שׁ.י *yasha*. Upon recording our discoveries, it might result in a list of English phrases like this:

> to free or liberate (or be freed, be liberated)
> to make wide, open, spacious (or be made spacious)
> to deliver or save (or be delivered or saved)
> to avenge (or be avenged)
> to gain victory
> to be endowed with salvation
> to preserve (or be preserved)
> to help, defend or rescue (or be helped, be defended, be rescued)

Next, we could look up the **noun forms** in Scripture that use the Hebrew root ע.שׁ.י *yasha*. Here's what we might come up with, depending on which English translations of the Bible we search:

> freedom, liberation
> deliverance, salvation, safety
> victory
> assistance, rescue, defense
> savior, liberator, deliverer, victor, rescuer, defender

Then, of course, to be thorough, we'd have to check out all the **adjective forms**:

> free, liberated,
> spacious, wide, open, abundant, sufficient
> delivered, saved, rescued, defended
> victorious
> safe

Our savior, Messiah Yeshua, holds all these meanings within the letters of His wonderful name! What a perfect picture of His ministry to us! If we combine this with the personal, covenant name of God which comprises the first half of the name *Yeshua*, then we add a whole other layer of meaning. According to ancient Jewish tradition and longstanding Christian scholarship, the personal name of God speaks of a Father who bends down toward humanity in great mercy, seeking a covenant relationship of faithful love with us.

The Woman Taken In Adultery by Giovanni Francesco Barbieri
(Guercino), 1621 (Dulwich Picture Gallery)

The dual nature of freedom in Christ

"Life more abundantly" is poured out upon believers in physical and spiritual ways.
John chapter 8 gives an example of how Yeshua set a woman free both ways at once –
from a sentence of capital punishment and from the bondage of sin.

Jesus was teaching in the temple when a woman caught in the act of adultery was brought before Him. Jesus delivered her from being stoned by her accusers – a group of scribes and Pharisees who were themselves guilty of the exact same sin. After the woman's accusers departed one by one, Jesus Himself set her free, forgiving her sins and saying, "Go and sin no more." The following exchange then occurred between Himself and other Jewish believers still present in the temple:

[31]Jesus therefore said to those Jews who had believed him, "If you remain in my word, then you are truly my disciples. [32]You will know the truth, and the truth will make you free."

[33]They answered him, "We are Abraham's seed and have never been in bondage to anyone. How do you say, 'You will be made free?'"

[34]Jesus answered them, "Most certainly I tell you, everyone who commits sin is the bondservant of sin. [35]A bondservant doesn't live in the house forever. A son remains forever. [36]If therefore the Son makes you free, you will be free indeed" (John 8, WEB).

                                    Lesson 3: "Core" meanings

Personal Reflections

What was the most surprising or interesting thing that occurred to you as you studied this particular lesson about the Hebrew name יֵשׁוּעַ *Yeshua*?

____

____

____

____

____

____

Recall that the core meaning of the Hebrew verbal root י.שׁ.ע *yasha* is *to make free* or *to be made free*. Consider Messiah Yeshua's ministry to the people of New Testament times as well as His ministry today. Write two verses from the B'rit Chadashah (New Testament) that show how Jesus sets His people free.

____

____

____

____

____

____

____

____

____

How did our LORD minister His Word directly to your heart through the passages you recorded above? What is He saying to you personally right now through Scripture?

____

____

____

____

____

____

____

Lesson 4

What about Greek?

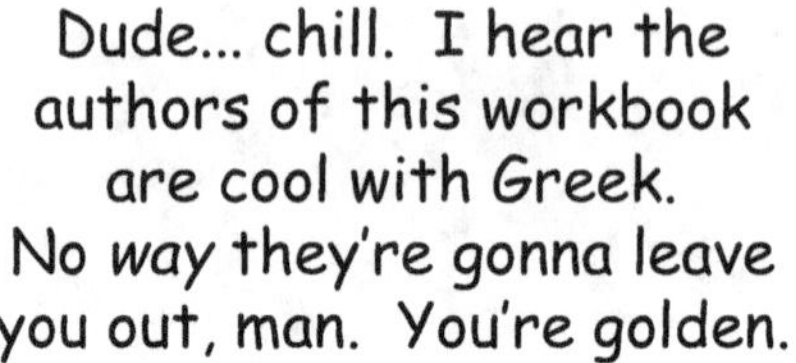

Well. I gotta admit, this Hebrew stuff we've been learning has been awesome. But... and I don't want to seem like I'm whining, here, but... what about Greek?
Dude... chill. I hear the authors of this workbook are cool with Greek. No way they're gonna leave you out, man. You're golden.

Lesson 4:
What about Greek?

The wondrous ministry of our Savior, Yeshua Ha Mashiach (Jesus the Christ) is resplendently pictured throughout the two Testaments of the Bible. His image and mark are *everywhere* in Scripture, for the Word of God is both a book and a Person, and that Person has never changed and never shall. The LORD is the one constant in an ever-changing universe. We should expect, then, to see the image of Yeshua from the Old Testament perfectly mirrored (and, in fact, revealed in sharper focus) in the New Testament. And this is indeed true. His eternal, unique character is unmistakably recognizable across both Testaments.

However, the moment that we attempt to trace the core meaning of a concept like יָשַׁע *yasha* *(to free, to save)* across the divide between Old and New Testaments, we hit an age-old wall: the barrier of language translation. (Thankfully, this barrier isn't insurmountable.)

The Old Testament was written in Hebrew – the covenant language of God's people Israel – while the New Testament was recorded in Greek – the lingua franca[1] of the secular Gentile world. Greek (like all languages) may use several different words to mean nearly the same thing. How can we be sure which of the several New Testament Greek verbs for *to free* or *to save* is a genuine match in meaning for the Hebrew verb *yasha* that we've been studying?

It turns out that Bible scholars have a variety of methods to find possible equivalent words between the two Testaments. One thing they do is study Old Testament passages that have the word *yasha* in them and see if they are quoted in the New Testament. Any Greek words meaning *to free* or *to save* in those New Testament passages are excellent candidates. Another technique is to look for verses that explicitly connect the concept of *yasha* to Yeshua's ministry in the context of the passage, then note which Greek verbs are used there. Sometimes, the New Testament doesn't even bother to translate Hebrew into Greek, instead opting to keep the Hebrew word intact and write out its pronunciation using Greek letters (a process called *transliteration*). Scholars will look for any such Hebrew-to-Greek transliterations that happen to have יָשַׁע *yasha* as their root.

In this and the following lessons, we will use some of these techniques to discover and explore three relevant Greek equivalents for the Hebrew root יָשַׁע *yasha*. Studying these Greek words in context will provide even more powerful, deep insight into the true meaning of our Savior's name.

---

1. **lingua franca** – a language that is adopted as a common language between speakers whose native languages are different. Following the conquests of Alexander the Great, Greek was adopted as a common language to facilitate diplomacy and trade between disparate nations all around the Mediterranean. Scholarly theories vary as to why God decided to ultimately preserve His B'rit Chadashah (Newer or Renewed Covenant) in the Greek language rather than in Hebrew, but one particular benefit of this decision is evident: it facilitated the rapid spread of the gospel into Gentile territories. Offering salvation to the Gentiles was "phase two" of God's plan to extend His covenant of saving grace to all men (where "phase one" was establishing His covenant of saving grace with Israel).

The New Testament word *hosanna*

Of the three New Testament Greek equivalents for the Hebrew root י.שׁ.ע *yasha* which we will be studying over the next few lessons, the Greek term ὡσαννά, *hosanna* (pronounced *ho-ssah-NAH*) maintains the closest relationship to the original Hebrew.

Hosanna is merely a Greek transliteration of a Hebrew term *hoshana* הוֹשַׁע נָא *(ho-shah NAH)*[2] meaning "Oh, save now!" or "Please deliver!" As we will soon learn, this ancient Jewish phrase has traditionally been directed to the Messiah. It serves simultaneously as a desperate cry for help and a shout of worshipful acclamation to God the Savior.

When we say that *hosanna* is just a transliteration, we mean that the New Testament writers Matthew, Mark and John all decided *not* to replace the Hebrew term with an equivalent Greek word having the same meaning as "save now" or "please save." Instead, they chose to "spell out" the original Hebrew pronunciation *hoshana* using Greek letters, resulting in *hosanna*. (An English speaker does something similar when he chooses to pronounce the Yiddish term "gesundheit" rather than translating it into its English equivalent, "bless you.") Matthew, Mark and John made a concerted effort to maintain the original pronunciation of *hoshana*. The only change they made was to replace the "sh" with an "s" because of Greek's inherent lack of a "sh" sound.

The fact that Matthew, Mark and John – Jewish men – all made a deliberate choice *not* to translate *hoshana* is highly significant. They felt the need to preserve the term as closely as possible to its pronunciation in the original Hebrew. They did this because the Hebrew *hoshana* was (and still is) a well-known term of great prophetic signficance in Jewish culture. Remember: these Jews' primary reason for recording the gospels back then was to explain all that they had seen and heard of Messiah's ministry to the rest of their Jewish brethren. Knowing their readers would instantly recognize and understand the term *hoshana*, they preserved it "as is" in the Greek. Perhaps, too, they were convinced that no single Greek replacement term could ever be capable of conveying the centuries of Jewish history and culture that are wrapped up in the Hebrew term *hoshana*.

What *hoshana* really means in Jewish culture

Not only is the Hebrew term *hoshana* packed with strong emotion as a standalone phrase (as we will soon see when we examine its Hebrew roots more closely), it also carries massive cultural and historical weight in traditional Judaism. *Hoshana* has always been specifically connected to the role and person of the Jewish Messiah. The fact that crowds of Jews in the New Testament shouted "Hoshana!" to Yeshua is what made that public acknowledgment of His Messiahship all the more credible – and astonishing. Soon, we'll take a look at these passages in the books of Matthew, Mark and John, and you'll see how astonishing it was, even for the people of that time.

---

2. The term also has an alternate Hebrew spelling of הוֹשִׁיעָה נָא *hoshiana* (as in Psalm 118:25), which is pronounced *ho-SHEE-ah NAH*. The meaning of "save now!" or "please, save!" is exactly the same in either spelling.

Since long before the time of Yeshua, a group of Psalms known as the *Hallel* has traditionally been sung during both Passover and the Feast of Tabernacles. It is within one of these Psalms, Psalm 118, that we find the primary reference to the Hebrew term *hoshana*. It is crucial for you to know **that the words of this psalm were traditionally understood to be a prayer for a coming Messiah who would save the house of Israel. These verses were always sung with this intention clearly in mind.** Here is the exact quote of those verses:

> O LORD, **please save us** [literally, "Hoshana!"]! O LORD, please prosper us! Blessed is He who comes in the name of the LORD! (Psalm 118:25-26a)

"Blessed is He who comes in the name of the LORD" is the age-old Jewish "code phrase" for **"Blessed is the Messiah."** It was a code phrase used for centuries to cry out in faith and hope, looking for the Messiah who would save God's people.

Yeshua – fulfillment of *Hoshana Rabbah*

Centuries before Yeshua ever walked the earth among us, the last (seventh) day of the Biblical Feast of Tabernacles was singled out and given the special titles "The Great Day" or "The Great Hoshana" (*Hoshana Rabbah* in Hebrew). On this day, all the people gathered in celebration, reciting the *Hallel*, singing the traditional annual prayer from Psalm 118, calling for the Messiah to come and save them all.

John 7:2 begins with the words "...the feast of Booths [Tabernacles] was at hand." A few verses later, we see that Yeshua attended this feast. On the seventh day of the feast – the "Great Day" *(Hoshana Rabbah)* –Yeshua made the earth-shaking declaration right there in front of everyone that He was indeed that Messiah!

> Now on the last day, the '**Great Day**' [i.e., *Hoshana Rabbah*] of the Feast [Tabernacles], Jesus stood and cried out, saying, "If any man is thirsty, let him come to Me and drink. He who believes in Me, as the Scripture has said, from his innermost being shall flow rivers of living water." But this He spoke of the Holy Spirit, whom those who believed in Him were to receive... (John 7:37-39).

Picture the scene. Massive crowds of people were gathered in Jerusalem, waving the branches of the *lulav* (a traditional bundle of tree branches waved during Tabernacles, of which the palm branch is the most prominent) and singing the words of Psalm 118, **"Save us, we beseech you [Hoshana]!** Blessed is He who comes in the name of the LORD!" The priests were pouring water in a ceremony at the foot of the altar, praying for rain (God's outpouring of His spirit and salvation). The traditional thinking at the time was that, through these songs and prayers of joyous celebration, the people would be "drawing" down upon themselves, like water, the very Holy Spirit of God. Everyone present understood that this feast wasn't just about physical water. The whole day was an obvious act of symbolism of the outpouring of the Holy Spirit and the saving of Israel.

So, when Yeshua stood up and made His declarations in *this* context, His statements were crystal clear to everyone. He was saying unmistakably that *He* was the source of living water. *He* was the source of the outpouring of the Holy Spirit. *He* was the one who had come from heaven to save them. *He* was the Messiah!

Did everyone really understand that Yeshua was claiming to be the Messiah?

Was the true meaning of Yeshua's declaration really that clear to everyone? Much of the crowd's response in John 7:40-53 proves that *everyone* understood the observance of *Hoshana Rabbah* to be all about looking for the coming Messiah. They understood exactly what Jesus meant when He made His symbolic statements about being the source of "living water." Grab your Bible and read John 7:40-53 again right now. They understood, all right.

To this very day, in places of Jewish worship all over the world, *lulavs* are waved and the *Hallel* is sung every year on the famous day of *Hoshana Rabbah* as the people look for a coming Messiah and pray for God's dual gifts of rain and Spirit. The symbolism of the term *hoshana* is still just as strong as ever.

In Messianic[3] circles, the symbolism of *hoshana* goes one step deeper. Messianic believers who choose to celebrate *Hoshana Rabbah* do so as a memorial of all that Yeshua accomplished during His first coming as well as all that He promises to accomplish in his second coming. These believers are blessed to be able to observe the Feast of Tabernacles while having a personal relationship with this Savior. They're not wondering who the Messiah is going to be. They know exactly who He is: *Yeshua ha Mashiach* (Jesus the Messiah), the very Yeshua of Nazareth portrayed throughout the New Testament.

---

3. **Messianic congregations** are mixed groups of Jews and Gentiles who believe Jesus is Messiah, Savior, Lord and God, and who worship Him together. They believe in being "born again," obtaining salvation through faith in Messiah's sacrificial death and resurrection, *purely* on the basis of the grace of God (*not* on the basis of human works, merit or effort). Messianic believers embrace both Old and New Testaments as "Torah" (that is, as God's divine and perfect "instruction") and celebrate the Biblical calendar (which includes God's feast days). They also permit and encourage celebrations of other significant Jewish life cycle events which are aligned with scriptural principles (Jewish weddings, bar/bat mitzvah celebrations, yizchor/memorials, etc). All those who attend, be they Jew or Gentile, are invited to freely participate in any observances to whatever extent they feel comfortable, but are never compelled to do so.

A closer look at the Hebrew spelling of *hoshana*

Let's study the term הוֹשַׁע נָא *hoshana* in Hebrew and try to get a glimpse into its core meaning. The phrase is actually composed of two separate words. Here they are, nice and large:

na   *hosha*

The first word (at the right) is the verb הוֹשַׁע *hosha* (pronounced *hō-SHAH*), meaning "Save!" or "Deliver!" This is nothing more than our old friend י.שׁ.ע *yasha (to free, to save)* in a particular form called the "imperative" (command form) as spoken to a masculine, singular object (such as a man).

The second word, נָא *na* (pronounced *NAH*) expresses the strongest possible emotion of entreaty. It is often translated "ah, now!" "oh, I beseech you!" or "we pray!" This is a word signalling a state of desperate need or desire. Picture a drowning man begging for someone to toss him a life preserver. Taken all together, the phrase *hoshana* might be translated "Save now! I beg you!"

By the way, did you happen to notice the root letters of י.שׁ.ע *yasha* in הוֹשַׁע *hosha*? We've colored in the root letters here:

hosha

Compare the root letters of the verb י.שׁ.ע *yasha* in the Hebrew origins of *Hosanna*, *Joshua*, and *Jesus*. They all convey the same core meaning of *to free, to save*.

hosha ("Save! Deliver!")

Y'hoshua (Joshua)
"The Lord is salvation"

Yeshua (Jeshua or Jesus)
"The Lord is salvation"

New Testament verses containing *hoshana/hosanna*

Nothing demonstrates the relationship between the Hebrew name *Yeshua* and His ministry as "the One who saves" better than reading about it in the context of Scripture. Following are all the verses in the New Testament containing the Greek transliteration ὡσαννά, *hosanna*. All of the passages we are about to study describe an event known as "The Triumphal Entry."

The Triumphal Entry was a remarkable event during which Yeshua rode into the city of Jerusalem when it was crowded with Jews from all nations there to celebrate the spring feast of Passover. The massive crowds acclaimed him as their Messiah, and He publicly received this acclamation.

This historic moment included all the hallmark prophetic symbols of *Hoshana Rabbah*, that last Great Day of the fall Feast of Tabernacles. It had folks waving palm branches. It had people shouting "Hoshana!" and "Son of David!" and "Blessed is he who comes in the name of the Lord!" There was only one problem with this Hoshana-Rabbah-like celebration. It happened **at the wrong time of year.** The Triumphal Entry occurred just before Passover, in the spring. This would be akin to a modern-day crowd gathering in New York's Times Square, wearing party hats, counting down from ten to one, and watching the ball drop – *on the Fourth of July.* Anyone who witnessed that would have to wonder what in the world was going on.

For centuries, scholars have grappled with the reason for the odd timing of this historic event, and many excellent theories have been put forth. Here's our favorite one: The premature public acclamation of the Messiah was a reflection of the people's misunderstanding of the timing of God's plan for Messiah's work. Those huge crowds were welcoming a Messiah whom they believed had come to deliver them *physically and politically* from the oppression of the Roman empire. (Where were those adoring crowds when Yeshua was being tried and crucified only days later?) These people weren't seeking spiritual deliverance, so they had little chance of recognizing it when it was occurring before their very eyes in the form of His sacrificial death.

God's timing in His plans for the human race is expressed symbolically in the order of His feasts. The **spring** feasts of the Lord – Passover, Unleavened Bread, Firstfruits, and Pentecost – were fulfilled by Yeshua's death, His burial, His resurrection, and the coming of the Indwelling Holy Spirit, respectively. The spring feast fulfillments speak of the *spiritual* deliverance from sin, of the salvation of the *soul.* They speak of the Kingdom of God established by a King who sits on the throne of the individual heart. This is the ministry of the *first* coming of Messiah.

In contrast, the **fall** feasts of the Lord speak of His *second* coming. The Day of Trumpets, the Day of Atonement and the Feast of Tabernacles are prophetic pictures of a *future, corporate* and very *public* ministry of Messiah. The Day of Trumpets is a prophecy about the Translation of Believers (aka the Rapture) – an earthshaking event that the entire world will witness. The Day of Atonement will be fulfilled by the future salvation of "all Israel," another publicly notable event. And the Feast of Tabernacles is a picture of the physical thousand-year reign of Yeshua over all the earth. It is only at Yeshua's *second* coming that Kingdom of God will express itself physically and publicly. It was this *physical, political* kingdom that the people were clamoring for during the springtime incident of the Triumphal Entry – out of synch with the timing of God's plan.

　　　　　　　　Lesson 4: What about Greek?

Ὡσαννὰ τῷ υἱῷ Δαυίδ... Ὡσαννὰ ἐν τοῖς ὑψίστοις!

Hosanna   to the   son   of David ...   Hosanna   in   the   highest

Ὡσαννὰ τῷ υἱῷ Δαυίδ...

Hosanna   to the   son   of David

⁶The disciples went and did just as Jesus commanded them, ⁷and brought the donkey and the colt, and laid their clothes on them; and he sat on them. ⁸A very great multitude spread their clothes on the road. Others cut branches from the trees and spread them on the road. ⁹The multitudes who went before him and who followed kept shouting, "**Hosanna** to the son of David! Blessed is he who comes in the name of the Lord! **Hosanna** in the highest!" ¹⁰When he had come into Jerusalem, all the city was stirred up, saying, "Who is this?" ¹¹The multitudes said, "This is the prophet, Jesus, from Nazareth of Galilee."

¹⁴The blind and the lame came to him in the temple, and he healed them. ¹⁵But when the chief priests and the scribes saw the wonderful things that he did, and the children who were crying in the temple and saying, "**Hosanna** to the son of David!" they were indignant, ¹⁶and said to him, "Do you hear what these are saying?" Jesus said to them, "Yes. Did you never read, 'Out of the mouth of babes and nursing babies you have perfected praise?'" (Matthew 21, WEB)

Context / Commentary

Note the three-fold Biblical (and Jewish cultural) references to the Messiah shouted by the crowd in acclamation of Yeshua of Nazareth: (1) "Hosanna/Hoshana" from Psalm 118 of the Hallel (traditionally sung on the day of Hoshana Rabbah while looking for the Messiah); (2) "the son of David" (the customary title for Messiah); and (3) "Blessed is He who comes in the name of the LORD" (the traditional blessing of the Messiah, also from Psalm 118).

καὶ οἱ προάγοντες καὶ οἱ ἀκολουθοῦντες ἔκραζον Ὡσαννά...

and   those   going before   and   those   following   were crying out   Hosanna

...Ὡσαννὰ ἐν τοῖς ὑψίστοις!

Hosanna   in   the   highest

[7]They brought the young donkey to Jesus, and threw their garments on it, and Jesus sat on it. [8]Many spread their garments on the way, and others were cutting down branches from the trees and spreading them on the road. [9]Those who went in front and those who followed cried out, "**Hosanna**! Blessed is he who comes in the name of the Lord! [10]Blessed is the kingdom of our father David that is coming in the name of the Lord! **Hosanna** in the highest!"

[11]Jesus entered into the temple in Jerusalem. When he had looked around at everything, it being now evening, he went out to Bethany with the twelve (Mark 11, WEB).

Context / Commentary

Again we see the three-fold Biblical (and traditional Jewish cultural) acclamation of Messiah: "Hosanna", "Blessed is he who comes in the name of the Lord, and "son of David" (by implication; "Blessed be the kingdom of our father David" means that the Messiah King was prophesied to arise out of the lineage of King David).

Of note is the word "our" in "our father David." Only a certain subgroup of people in Israel could claim any ancestry to King David (Yeshua was one of them). It was far more common for a Jew to call himself a "son of Abraham." There are two possible reasons for this unusual "our father David" statement. Perhaps the people were demonstrating a unified willingness to subjugate themselves under this upcoming King who would reign from David's ancient throne (thus calling David their figurative father). Or, perhaps those shouting in this specific verse happened to be of those Judeans who had physically descended from the house of David. This option is less probable, but if true, it would further color the meaning of their shouted praises. Yeshua the political Savior (as they believed him to be) was truly "one of their own." Already holding somewhat elevated positions in society, these sons of David would have coveted the yet higher clout that they stood to gain by being physical relatives of this up-and-coming king.

‘Ωσαννά, εὐλογημένος ὁ ἐρχόμενος ἐν ὀνόματι Κυρίου!

Hosanna   *blessed is*   *the [one]*   *coming*   *in [the]*   *name*   *of [the] Lord*

¹²On the next day a great multitude had come to the feast. When they heard that Jesus was coming to Jerusalem, ¹³they took the branches of the palm trees, and went out to meet him and cried out, "**Hosanna**! Blessed is he who comes in the name of the Lord, the King of Israel!" ¹⁴Jesus, having found a young donkey, sat on it. As it is written, ¹⁵"Don't be afraid, daughter of Zion. Behold, your King comes, sitting on a donkey's colt." ¹⁶His disciples didn't understand these things at first, but when Jesus was glorified, then they remembered that these things were written about him, and that they had done these things to him. ¹⁷The multitude therefore that was with him when he called Lazarus out of the tomb, and raised him from the dead, was testifying about it. ¹⁸For this cause also the multitude went and met him, because they heard that he had done this sign. ¹⁹The Pharisees therefore said among themselves, "See how you accomplish nothing. Behold, the world has gone after him" (John 12, WEB).

Context / Commentary

The themes of "Hosanna," "Blessed is He who comes in the name of the Lord," and "the Kingdom" (by implication, that of the "son of David") are reflected in John's testimony of the event. The leadership and authority of Yeshua was recognized not only by those who praised Him, but by those who opposed him, albeit begrudgingly (v. 19).

Entrée de Jésus-Christ dans Jérusalem (Entry of Jesus Christ into Jerusalem) by Félix Louis Leullier, mixed media, 1858

The power of the term *Hoshana* endures to this day

To this day, in Conservative[4] and Orthodox synagogues, the following phrases are sung or spoken by the congregation every year on the day of Hoshana Rabbah. All of these phrases may be found interspersed in the form of congregational responses to the many prayers and Scripture readings of the service. The humble, plaintive, desperate nature of the prayers is absolutely heartwrenching.

Hoshana! Please save – for Your sake, our God! Hoshana!
Hoshana! Please save – for Your sake, our Creator! Hoshana!
Hoshana! Please save – for Your sake, our Redeemer! Hoshana!
Hoshana! Please save – for Your sake, our Attender! Hoshana!
Bring salvation now. Please bring salvation now...
Please God, please! Hoshana! Save now, for You are our Father...
Hoshana! save now, forgive now, bring us success now, and save us, God our Strength...
Show mercy, please, to the congregation of Jeshurun's[5] flock;
forgive and pardon their iniquities; and save us, God of our salvation...
Open the gates of heaven, and Your bountiful treasure may You open for us.
Save us, do not let contention be prolonged, and save us, God of our salvation...
Open your bountiful treasure to satisfy a thirsty soul with water...[6]

---

4   **conservative** – a form of Judaism which seeks to preserve Jewish tradition and ritual but has a more flexible approach to the interpretation of the law than Orthodox Judaism. Conservative Judaism, as a whole, does not currently accept Yeshua as Messiah. Neither does Orthodox Judaism, as a whole.

5   **Jeshurun** – an affectionate name God uses in Scripture to admonish Israel when she has sinned and He is calling her to return to righteousness.

6   **water** – This traditional Hoshana Rabbah prayer for water is evidently not just about physical water or rain. In fact, it was in response to this prayer that Yeshua made His startling claim – on the very day of Hoshana Rabbah – that He was that source of "living water," i.e., the Messiah (John 7:37-39).

Personal Reflections

What was the most surprising or interesting thing that occurred to you as you studied this particular lesson about the Hebrew name יֵשׁוּעַ *Yeshua?*

____

____

____

____

____

Think about a time in your own life that you (figuratively) cried "Hoshana!" to God in a desperate plea for Him to save you. How did His response teach you about the character (i.e., name) of Yeshua? Did that response change your own character?

____

____

____

____

____

____

____

____

How did our Lord minister His Word directly to your heart through the passages you recorded above? What is He saying to you personally right now through Scripture?

____

____

____

____

____

____

Lesson 5

The naming of the infant Yeshua

The Annunciation (L'annonciation), James Tissot, 1886-1894, Brooklyn Museum.

The angel said to her, "Don't be afraid, Mary,
for you have found favor with God.
Behold, you will conceive in your womb,
and bring forth a son,
and will call his name Jesus."

Luke 1:30–31 WEB

 Lesson 5: The naming of the infant Yeshua

Lesson 5:
The naming of the infant Yeshua

In our ongoing search for Greek words in the New Testament which have a scriptural relationship with the name *Yeshua*, the passages that describe why He was given that name are essential for study. In these passages, we discover one Greek verb that consistently arises: the word σῴζω *sozo* (pronounced *SŌ-zō* [1]), whose core meaning is *to make safe* or *to be made safe*.

Interestingly, the core meaning of σῴζω *sozo* isn't an exact equivalent for the Hebrew verb יָשַׁע *yasha*. Recall that *yasha's* core meaning is *to set free, to place in wide open freedom*. *Sozo* doesn't actually include this concept of *wide open space* in its core meaning, but *sozo* does describe the sorts of activities that end up with the same results as *yasha*. Remember: when we studied *yasha* a few lessons back, we learned that someone who has been *set free* from a situation may be said to be *saved* or *delivered*. That's why we often see *yasha* translated *to save* or *to deliver* in our English Bibles. In contrast, the Greek verb *sozo* actually has *to save, to deliver* as its core meaning. You can see why the New Testament writers went with *sozo*. Whether you're reading about *yasha* in the TaNaCH or *sozo* in the B'rit Chadashah[2], when it comes to describing God's activity in the life of the believer, the practical results are identical.

Sozo differs in yet another way from *yasha*. The New Testament writers found intriguing ways to expand the meaning of *sozo* to many fresh, new contexts as they described the life and ministry of Yeshua. These diverse usages will be illuminated later in this lesson as we trace the roots of this word through Scripture. You'll see that *sozo* – with its wellspring of rich and varied applications – is a verb well suited to describe the multi-faceted aspects of Yeshua's ministry.

Now, let's turn our attention to the wondrous gospel accounts about **the naming of the infant Yeshua.**

---

1. Scholars are divided on how σῴζω *sozo* was actually pronounced thousands of years ago (since we have no audio recordings from that time to prove things one way or the other). Some linguists think that σῴζω was pronounced with a "dz" sound: *SO-dzo*. Others say it was pronounced with a "zd" sound: *SO-zdo*. In modern Biblical Greek classes, most professors consider it acceptable to use a regular "z" sound: *SO-zo*. (Don't be alarmed if you hear a Greek professor using a slightly different pronunciation than, say, your pastor does. Varying Biblical Greek pronunciation among people of different academic backgrounds is a common phenomenon.)

2. **B'rit Chadashah** – Hebrew for *new/newer/renewed covenant*, i.e., the New Testament. The term *B'rit Chadashah* is commonly used by Messianic Jews and by people whose native language is Hebrew.

In the following passages, we have bolded and underlined references to the naming of Jesus as well as any words which spring from the same root as the Greek σώζω *sozo*. The scriptural connection between this root and the name *Yeshua* (Jesus) is striking.

[26]Now in the sixth month, the angel Gabriel was sent from God to a city of Galilee, named Nazareth, [27]to a virgin pledged to be married to a man whose name was Joseph, of the house of David. The virgin's name was Mary. [28]Having come in, the angel said to her, "Rejoice, you highly favored one! The Lord is with you. Blessed are you among women!" [29]But when she saw him, she was greatly troubled at the saying, and considered what kind of salutation this might be. [30]The angel said to her, "Don't be afraid, Mary, for you have found favor with God. [31]Behold, you will conceive in your womb, and bring forth a son, and **will call his name 'Jesus.'** [32]He will be great, and will be called the Son of the Most High. The Lord God will give him the throne of his father, David, [33]and he will reign over the house of Jacob forever. There will be no end to his Kingdom." [34]Mary said to the angel, "How can this be, seeing I am a virgin?" [35]The angel answered her, "The Holy Spirit will come on you, and the power of the Most High will overshadow you. Therefore also the holy one who is born from you will be called the Son of God. [36]Behold, Elizabeth, your relative, also has conceived a son in her old age; and this is the sixth month with her who was called barren. [37]For everything spoken by God is possible." [38]Mary said, "Behold, the handmaid of the Lord; be it to me according to your word." The angel departed from her.

[39]Mary arose in those days and went into the hill country with haste, into a city of Judah, [40]and entered into the house of Zacharias and greeted Elizabeth. [41]It happened, when Elizabeth heard Mary's greeting, that the baby leaped in her womb, and Elizabeth was filled with the Holy Spirit. [42]She called out with a loud voice, and said, "Blessed are you among women, and blessed is the fruit of your womb! [43]Why am I so favored, that the mother of my Lord should come to me? [44]For behold, when the voice of your greeting came into my ears, the baby leaped in my womb for joy! [45]Blessed is she who believed, for there will be a fulfillment of the things which have been spoken to her from the Lord!"

[46]Mary said, "My soul magnifies the Lord.

[47]My spirit has rejoiced in God my **Savior**,

[48]for he has looked at the humble state of his handmaid. For behold, from now on, all generations will call me blessed (Luke 1, WEB).

The name *Yeshua* is told to Yoseph by an angel

[18]Now the birth of Jesus Christ was like this; for after his mother, Mary, was engaged to Joseph, before they came together, she was found pregnant by the Holy Spirit. [19]Joseph, her husband, being a righteous man, and not willing to make her a public example, intended to put her away secretly. [20]But when he thought about these things, behold, an angel of the Lord appeared to him in a dream, saying, "Joseph, son of David, don't be afraid to take to yourself Mary, your wife, for that which is conceived in her is of the Holy Spirit. [21]She shall bring forth a son. **You shall call his name Jesus**, for it is he who shall **save** his people from their sins." [22]Now all this has happened, that it might be fulfilled which was spoken by the Lord through the prophet, saying, [23]"Behold, the virgin shall be with child, and shall bring forth a son. They shall call his name Immanuel;" which is, being interpreted, "God with us." [24]Joseph arose from his sleep, and did as the angel of the Lord commanded him, and took his wife to himself; [25]and didn't know her sexually until she had brought forth her firstborn son. **He named him Jesus** (Matthew 1, WEB).

An angel tells shepherds of the birth of a Savior

[8]There were shepherds in the same country staying in the field, and keeping watch by night over their flock. [9]Behold, an angel of the Lord stood by them, and the glory of the Lord shone around them, and they were terrified. [10]The angel said to them, "Don't be afraid, for behold, I bring you good news of great joy which will be to all the people. [11]For there is born to you, this day, in the city of David, a **Savior**, who is Christ the Lord. [12]This is the sign to you: you will find a baby wrapped in strips of cloth, lying in a feeding trough." [13]Suddenly, there was with the angel a multitude of the heavenly army praising God, and saying, [14]"Glory to God in the highest, on earth peace, good will toward men" (Luke 2, WEB).

A quick note about the next passage. From the time of Moses until now, the official naming of Jewish male infants has been done at a ceremony known as *b'rit milah* (circumcision), which God commands in His Torah to be performed on the eighth day of the child's life. Following this, the mother waits the Torah-prescribed number of days before she may perform her own *mikveh* (ceremonial immersion in water) in order to be ceremonially fit to re-enter the temple to present such offerings as the "sacrifice for the firstborn." It was during Miriam's (Mary's) visit to the temple that the righteous Shimon (Simeon) uttered his wonderful prophecy under the influence of the Holy Spirit.

Yeshua is officially named. Shimon prophesies.

²¹When eight days were fulfilled for the circumcision of the child, **his name was called Jesus**, which was given by the angel before he was conceived in the womb.

²²When the days of their purification according to the law of Moses were fulfilled, they brought him up to Jerusalem, to present him to the Lord ²³(as it is written in the law of the Lord, "Every male who opens the womb shall be called holy to the Lord"), ²⁴and to offer a sacrifice according to that which is said in the law of the Lord, "A pair of turtledoves, or two young pigeons."

²⁵Behold, there was a man in Jerusalem whose name was Simeon. This man was righteous and devout, looking for the consolation of Israel, and the Holy Spirit was on him. ²⁶It had been revealed to him by the Holy Spirit that he should not see death before he had seen the Lord's Christ. ²⁷He came in the Spirit into the temple. When the parents brought in the child, Jesus, that they might do concerning him according to the custom of the law, ²⁸then he received him into his arms, and blessed God, and said,

²⁹"Now you are releasing your servant, Master, according to your word, in peace; ³⁰for my eyes have seen your **salvation**, ³¹which you have prepared before the face of all peoples; ³²a light for revelation to the nations, and the glory of your people Israel" (Luke 2, WEB).

These wonderful, blessed accounts are packed with descriptions of the character and nature of Messiah Yeshua. Not only do we see the concept of salvation in the Greek word *sozo, to save* intertwined with the name *Yeshua*, but we also see mentions of the "son of David" theme, which is connected with the Hebrew *yasha, to set free (to save)* through the famous phrase "Hoshana to the son of David."

"Joseph, of the house of David" (Luke 1:27)

"the throne of his father, David" (Luke 1:32)

"Joseph, son of David" (Matthew 1:20)

"in the city of David" (Luke 2:11)

A closer look at sozo

The Greek word σῴζω *sozo*, has a core meaning of *to bring to safety*. It has a surprisingly wide variety of applications in the New Testament. Check out this list of possible translations (not exhaustive!) according to *Strong's Dictionary*, the *New American Standard Concordance* and *Thayer's Lexicon:*

- to deliver out of physical or spiritual danger and into safety
- to rescue from destruction
- to remove from the power of sin and place in divine provision
- to cure, to make well, to make whole (physically or spiritually)
- to keep safe and sound, to preserve
- to restore, to recover to full prosperity or health
- to deliver from the penalties of the Messianic judgment
- to save from evils which obstruct the reception of Messiah's deliverance
- to make one a partaker of salvation by Messiah
- to deliver from the punitive wrath of God

The root of the verb *sozo* can express itself as a noun, too, in Greek. The noun form also has diverse usages, as the Bible dictionaries show:

- safety
- welfare
- prosperity
- deliverance
- defense or defender
- preservation
- salvation

How does σῴζω *sozo* reflect the diverse ministries of our Messiah? Below are just a few examples of *sozo* in the New Testament, with each instance bolded and underlined for your convenience.

When *sozo* means "to heal" from a malady

[20]Behold, a woman who had an issue of blood for twelve years came behind Him and touched the fringe of his garment; [21]for she said within herself, "If I just touch his garment, I will be **made well**." [22]But Jesus, turning around and seeing her, said, "Daughter, cheer up! Your faith has **made you well**." And the woman was **made well** from that hour (Matthew 9, WEB).

When *sozo* means "to heal" from demonic possession

[35]People went out to see what had happened. They came to Jesus and found the man from whom the demons had gone out, sitting at Jesus' feet, clothed and in his right mind; and they were afraid. [36]Those who saw it told them how he who had been possessed by demons was **healed** (Luke 8, WEB).

When *sozo* means "to physically preserve or rescue"

[28]Peter answered him and said, "Lord, if it is you, command me to come to you on the waters." [29]He said, "Come!" Peter stepped down from the boat and walked on the waters to come to Jesus. [30]But when he saw that the wind was strong, he was afraid, and beginning to sink, he cried out, saying, "Lord, **save** me!" (Matthew 14, WEB)

[19]For in those days there will be oppression, such as there has not been the like from the beginning of the creation which God created until now, and never will be. [20]Unless the Lord had shortened the days, no flesh would have been **saved**; but for the sake of the chosen ones, whom he picked out, he shortened the days (Mark 13, WEB).

When *sozo* means "to preserve one's position" (of honor)

[15]...but [womankind] will be **saved** through her childbearing, if they continue in faith, love, and sanctification with sobriety (1 Timothy 2, WEB).

When *sozo* means "to preserve spiritually"

[8]for by grace you have been **saved** through faith, and that not of yourselves; it is the gift of God, [9]not of works, that no one would boast" (Ephesians 2, WEB).

   Lesson 5: The naming of the infant Yeshua

In Scripture, "name" also means "character"

Since you began reading this book, you've learned a lot about the Hebrew and Greek words associated with the name of Yeshua. Right here is a great place to take a pause. Let's stop for a moment, review what we've learned, and try to drink it all in.

It's important that we do this. We need to recall the reason we're studying the name of Yeshua in the first place. It's because, throughout the Bible, a person's *name* is more than some random collection of syllables used to specify an entity. In Scripture, a *name* is a description of a person's *character*. While this is true of humans, it is *especially* true of God, the Unchanging and Eternal One, the Creator of the Universe. Verse after verse speak of His *name*, and psalms and prayers ask for His justice and mercy to be performed "for the sake of Your name." In fact, in traditional Judaism, the Hebrew personal name of God is seen as so intertwined with the very Person of God – so holy – that it isn't uttered aloud, nor is it written fully spelled out except in sacred texts.

So, let's review all the information we've gathered up to this point. In Lesson 1, we learned that the name *Jesus* is really *Yeshua*, which is actually *Y'hoshua*, meaning "the Lord is salvation." What a statement of God's character, right there.

Lesson 2 taught us that the people named *Yeshua* in the TaNaCH were spiritual symbols of the roles that Messiah would fulfill in history. High priest, spiritual head, leader of God's people out of exile and into freedom, dispenser of God's treasures, defender of God's people, and leader of God's people into the promised land are just a few of these roles.

In Lesson 3, we saw that the root letters of *Yeshua* included the Hebrew root *yasha*, whose core meaning is *to free*, but in application can mean *to save, deliver, avenge, gain victory, preserve, defend, rescue, help, liberate*. What a powerful picture of God's ministry these words portray.

Lesson 4 brought us into the New Testament, where we began to attempt to find equivalent Greek terms for the Hebrew *yasha*. We were blessed to find the Greek transliteration *hosanna* of the Hebrew *hoshana*, "Save now, we pray!" – the famous code term directed to the Messiah, Son of David. The passages of B'rit Chadashah containing *hosanna* perfectly connect the core meaning of *yasha* with His name, *Yeshua*, as well as His role as Son of David, King of Israel.

The current lesson looked into the passages describing the naming of Jesus and there discovered another Greek word closely related to our Messiah: *sozo, to save*. The varied applications of this word throughout the New Testament really expand the description of Yeshua's ministry and character. He not only *saves* the soul from hell, but He *heals* from illness or demonic oppression. He *preserves* a person's honor as they walk closely with Him. He *rescues* his children from physical danger. And He *delivers* us from the permanency of physical death.

Take a moment now to prayerfully consider the wonders of His name, then write your thoughts on the Personal Reflections page at the end of the lesson.

The Presentation of Jesus in the Temple (La présentation de Jésus au Temple), James Tissot, 1886-1894.

Now you are releasing your servant, Master,
according to your word, in peace; for my eyes have seen
*your **salvation**, which you have prepared before the*
face of all peoples; a light for revelation to the nations,
and the glory of your people Israel.

The prophecy of Shimon
under the influence of the Holy Spirit
Luke 2:29–32 WEB

　　　　Lesson 5: The naming of the infant Yeshua

Personal Reflections

What was the most surprising or interesting thing that occurred to you as you studied this particular lesson about the Hebrew name יְשׁוּעַ *Yeshua?*

In your own life, have there been times that Yeshua saved you from a physical danger or illness? Did He lift an oppressive spirit from your shoulders? Write a thank-you to Him now for a few of those times that stand out most in your memory.

Lesson 6

Another possible Greek equivalent for the Hebrew *yasha*

Jesus Speaks Near the Treasury (Jésus parle près du trésor), James Tissot, 1886-1896.

Jesus therefore said to those Jews who had believed him,
"If you remain in my word, then you are truly my disciples.
You will know the truth, and the truth will make you free."

John 8:31-32 WEB

Lesson 6:
Another possible Greek equivalent for the Hebrew *yasha*

In our quest to understand the name Yeshua from the standpoint of New Testament Greek, we've used two techniques so far. In Lesson 4, we found a Greek transliteration of the Hebrew יָשַׁע *yasha, to free,* in the word ὡσαννά *hosanna,* and then we studied all its contexts. In Lesson 5, we read all the Scripture passages describing the reason the infant Yeshua was so named and discovered that the root of the Greek verb σῴζω *sozo, to save,* was prominently featured in those passages. The two techniques used in Lessons 4 and 5 are highly reliable, for in them the divinely inspired Word of God points us *directly* to Greek words associated with the Person of Yeshua.

A third technique – to scan the Greek dictionary for any verb that might have a close core meaning to that of the Hebrew *yasha* – is the technique which will be used here in Lesson 6. This technique is inherently less certain than the other two. We'll explain why.

At first glance, it seems a fairly simple process: we crack open a New Testament Greek Concordance and Dictionary (or, better yet, we use a searchable online or desktop software version) and just start scanning for the definition *to free.* Several Greek verbs come up in the results. But which one really means the same as the Hebrew *yasha?* We learn that there are many *kinds* of freedom: legal, financial, ceremonial, ethical, physical, spiritual. Here's where the study gets less cut and dried. We must carefully read every context of every verb and methodically whittle down our selections to those we think *most closely* connect with the meaning of *Yeshua.*

In order to compile this particular lesson, we conducted the exercise above and arrived at the Greek verb ἐλευθερόω *eleutheroō* (pronounced *el-yoo-ther-AH-oh*): *to set free, to liberate.* We realize, of course, that there are several other Greek words which might also be suitable candidates for equivalents of *yasha,* but we believe that *eleutheroō* is the closest fit for Yeshua's ministry, based on what we read of *eleutheroō's* Biblical usages.

We'll confess right up front that this technique involves a certain amount of individual judgment (i.e., "bias"). Individual bias *always* comes into play in *all* translation work. Bias simply cannot be avoided; therefore, it's best that we acknowledge its ever-lurking presence in order to remain on the alert for it. We're all human, right? In our less-than-perfect efforts at translation, we have to make our best human judgments, and we sometimes inadvertently introduce a certain amount of "skew" or "spin." Why does this occur? Because we humans tend to find what we *intend* to find. We see what we *expect* to see. In a way, it's amazing that we ever learn anything new, especially things of the Spirit. It takes an ongoing, miraculous act of God for us to fully grasp and absorb all that God truly means in Scripture. There's an excellent reason for the prayer in Psalm 119:18, "Open my eyes, that I may see wondrous things out of Your law." The miraculous phenomenon of eye opening is also described when Yeshua "opened their minds, that they might understand the Scriptures" (Luke 24:45). Since we are so dependent on God's supernatural power for comprehension of His Word, we should approach Scripture with worshipful awe and humility.

That being said, perhaps you would still like to try this technique of finding Greek equivalents for the Hebrew *yasha* on your own.[1] If you do decide to do this exercise, you might come up with a completely different Greek equivalent for *yasha* than we did. That's not only *okay* – it's *great!* God could be showing you something in His Word that we totally missed.

This sort of thing happens all the time, of course. One believer notices one thing in a Bible passage, while something altogether different jumps out at someone else as they read. That's what makes group Bible study so wonderful; the Holy Spirit works through the Body of believers to minister to each other by diverse gifts – and through diverse points of view.

When it comes to matters not essential to salvation itself, we don't all have to understand everything in Scripture the exact same way.   In fact, it's probably better that we don't, for the Word is living and active, constantly redirecting and customizing His emphasis upon certain issues as He individually addresses the needs of specific believers in certain places at certain times. We should graciously grant other believers the *freedom* to listen for God's voice of interpretation as they study Scripture. (After all, the lesson we are studying now is all about the Greek word for *freedom!*) We can relax and trust the Holy Spirit to "lead us into all truth" – as long as our intentions are pure: to keep His Word with a whole heart full of grace, love, humility and gratitude.

Let's dive in now and learn about ἐλευθερόω *eleutherŏō, to free.*

The meanings of *eleutherŏō, to free*

The Greek word ἐλευθερόω *eleutherŏō,* has a core meaning of *to free.* Here's a list of possible translations according to *Strong's Dictionary,* the *New American Standard Concordance* and *Thayer's Lexicon:*

- to set free, to liberate, to deliver
- to release from bondage
- to remove the restrictions or dominion of sin / darkness
- to exempt from liability (moral, ceremonial, or mortal)

The following pages contain the passages in New Testament Scripture where the Greek verb *eleutherŏō* is used. We have also underlined any words in these contexts in which its verbal root happens to be expressed as an adjective or noun. These passages are beautiful and awe-inspiring, and we hope you will enjoy reading them as much as we enjoyed finding them.

---

1. By the way, we encourage you to prayerfully consider doing this kind of word-study exploration on your own as much as possible, rather than relying on a rabbi or pastor to do it for you. That way, if you're concerned about bias, you at least give yourself the chance to see Scripture in its original languages from a clean perspective. Later, you can compare your findings to that of your teacher or whatever commentary you are studying and see what you think then. Two human perspectives on a topic are usually better than one, but the Holy Spirit's perspective as He ministers directly to you in your personal study time supercedes any human perspective. You can rely on Him to be one-hundred-percent correct and bias-free!

$$...καὶ \quad ἡ \quad ἀλήθεια \quad ἐλευθερώσει \quad ὑμᾶς.$$

and   the   truth   will set free   you

$$πῶς \quad σὺ \quad λέγεις \quad ὅτι \quad Ἐλεύθεροι \quad γενήσεσθε;$$

how   you   say   free   you will become?

$$ἐὰν \quad οὖν \quad ὁ \quad Υἱὸς \quad ὑμᾶς \quad ἐλευθερώσῃ, \quad ὄντως \quad ἐλεύθεροι \quad ἔσεσθε.$$

if   therefore   the   Son   you   shall set free   indeed   free   you will be

[31]Jesus therefore said to those Jews who had believed him, "If you remain in my word, then you are truly my disciples. [32]You will know the truth, and the truth will make you **free**." [33]They answered him, "We are Abraham's seed, and have never been in bondage to anyone. How do you say, 'You will be made **free**?'"

[34]Jesus answered them, "Most certainly I tell you, everyone who commits sin is the bondservant of sin. [35]A bondservant doesn't live in the house forever. A son remains forever. [36]If therefore the Son **makes you free**, you will be **free** indeed. (John 8, WEB).

Context / Commentary

Here Yeshua was speaking to those gathered in the temple to hear Him teach. In this discourse, Yeshua clarified that the kind of freedom He was offering was freedom from sin. This discourse occurred just after He freed the woman caught in adultery. He not only set the woman free from physical death – the capital punishment of stoning – but, more importantly, He set her spiritually free from sin.

ἐλευθερωθέντες δὲ ἀπὸ τῆς ἀμαρτίας...

having been set free   now   from   sin

νυνὶ δέ ἐλευθερωθέντες ἀπὸ τῆς ἀμαρτίας...

now   however   having been set free   from   sin

[17]But thanks be to God, that, whereas you were bondservants of sin, you became obedient from the heart to that form of teaching whereunto you were delivered. [18]**Being made free** from sin, you became bondservants of righteousness...

[22]But now, **being made free** from sin, and having become servants of God, you have your fruit of sanctification, and the result of eternal life. [23]For the wages of sin is death, but the [gift] of God is eternal life in Christ Jesus our Lord (Romans 6, WEB).

Context / Commentary

In this letter to the believers in Rome, Rav Shaul (Rabbi Saul / The Apostle Paul) contrasts the unrelenting, oppressive slavery of sin against the peaceable servitude of God. Serving God is a whole-hearted, voluntary "enslavement of love" which paradoxically results in a blessed life of pure, real freedom. Paul makes it clear throughout this letter that the only source of real freedom and eternal life is "in Messiah Yeshua our Adonai" (v. 23 above). Eternal life is granted purely as a gift to any believer with "no strings attached." Messiah's gift of eternal life is completely independent of how perfectly – or imperfectly – the believer is able to keep God's good and holy commandments ("instruction" or "teaching", v. 17).

Believers who truly love their Father will discover that they can't help but keep on trying to do exactly as He instructs, though. This is as an outward reaction spilling over from our affection, loyalty and gratitude toward Him as a result of already having received His salvation. In other words, God's gift of salvation is the initial <u>cause</u> of the believer's transformation (from the inside out). Then, any obedience on the part of the believer is merely the visible <u>effect</u>, or result, of that innermost transformation. This "obedient walk of grace" can only spring from a believer's overwhelming love for a Savior who has <u>previously</u> forgiven him and who has <u>already</u> reached down from heaven to deliver this undeserving sinner from death and hell – this while he was yet helplessly dead in his sins and had no capability of earning or meriting this act of deliverance. As Yeshua Himself puts it, one who has been forgiven much loves much (Luke 7:47).

 Lesson 6: Another possible Greek equivalent for the Hebrew *yasha*

...νόμος τοῦ Πνεύματος τῆς ζωῆς ἐν Χριστῷ Ἰησοῦ ἠλευθέρωσέν...

the law   of the   Spirit   of   life   in   Messiah   Yeshua   has set free

...ἡ κτίσις ἐλευθερωθήσεται... εἰς τὴν ἐλευθερίαν τῆς δόξης...

the   creation   will be set free   into   the   freedom   of the   glory

[1]There is therefore now no condemnation to those who are in Christ Jesus, who don't walk according to the flesh, but according to the Spirit. [2]For the law of the Spirit of life in Christ Jesus **made me free** from the law of sin and of death... [5]For those who live according to the flesh set their minds on the things of the flesh, but those who live according to the Spirit, the things of the Spirit. [6]For the mind of the flesh is death, but the mind of the Spirit is life and peace; [7]because the mind of the flesh is hostile towards God; for it is not subject to God's law, neither indeed can it be. [8]Those who are in the flesh can't please God...

[19]For the creation waits with eager expectation for the children of God to be revealed. [20]For the creation was subjected to vanity, not of its own will, but because of him who subjected it, in hope [21]that the creation itself also **will be delivered** from the bondage of decay into the **liberty** of the glory of the children of God. [22]For we know that the whole creation groans and travails in pain together until now. [23]Not only so, but ourselves also, who have the first fruits of the Spirit, even we ourselves groan within ourselves, waiting for adoption, the redemption of our body (Romans 8, WEB).

Context / Commentary

This passage from Romans 8 requires some clarification. Here, Paul speaks of a "law" of "sin and death." In Greek, the word νόμος nomos, "law," may be translated "a general principle describing an observable, long-proven phenomenon" – as in the "law" of gravity. However, nomos is also used to describe God's perfect, holy, righteous and unchanging "Law" – i.e., His Torah, or "instruction." Paul tends to use the word nomos both ways, which can lead to confusion. To clarify, when Paul uses the phrase "the law of sin and death" (verse 2), he's talking about the general principle that has governed everything on this planet since the inception of original sin: the undeniable fact that all things die, all decay, all suffer, all struggle, all groan. (In contrast, in verses 3, 4 and 7, Paul switches over to use nomos in the sense of God's good, holy Torah of life, whose "righteousness is fulfilled" in those who "walk in the Spirit"). The entire context of the chapter makes it clear that Messiah provides miraculous liberation from the "general principle" that "sin begets death," (not liberation from the Holy Law which He Himself has written for His people with the promise of long life and blessing to all who obey it). Note that Messiah promises to liberate not only us believers from our bodies of decay, but eventually the whole of creation.

Τῇ ἐλευθερίᾳ ἡμᾶς Χριστὸς ἠλευθέρωσεν...

in   freedom   us   Messiah   has set free

Ὑμεῖς γὰρ ἐπ' ἐλευθερίᾳ ἐκλήθητε, ἀδελφοί...

You   for   to   freedom   were called   brothers

...μόνον μὴ τὴν ἐλευθερίαν εἰς ἀφορμὴν τῇ σαρκί...

but   not   the   freedom   for   an opportunity   to the   flesh

[1]Stand firm therefore in the **liberty** by which Christ **has made us free**, and don't be entangled again with a yoke of bondage. [2]Behold, I, Paul, tell you that if you receive circumcision, Christ will profit you nothing. [3]Yes, I testify again to every man who receives circumcision, that he is a debtor to do the whole law. [4]You are alienated from Christ, you who desire to be justified by the law. You have fallen away from grace...

[13]For you, brothers, were called for **freedom**. Only don't use your **freedom** for gain to the flesh, but through love be servants to one another. [14]For the whole law is fulfilled in one word, in this: "You shall love your neighbor as yourself." [15]But if you bite and devour one another, be careful that you don't consume one another (Galatians 5, WEB).

Context / Commentary

The believing community to whom Rabbi Paul wrote this letter was facing a multi-frontal spiritual attack. First, some in the congregation were being tempted to return to idolatry because of their lifelong habits of keeping pagan feast days (4:8-10). Second, there was bitter infighting in the group (5:15). Third, some Jewish men were errantly teaching the congregation that circumcision was absolutely required for salvation of the soul. God's Torah itself never stated that circumcision was a requirement for salvation, not at all. Rather, it was commanded to be done only as an outward sign of God's covenant of loving grace with Israel. Salvation has always been a free gift offered by grace through faith, even back in Old Testament times (Noah found "grace"; Abraham pleased God by "faith"; etc.). Paul was stating in this letter that if all that was required for salvation was mere obedience to Torah, then Yeshua's death was completely unnecessary; therefore, belief in Messiah would profit nothing. Circumcision in itself is certainly no bad thing, but legalism is. "Legalism" means "a method of attempting to merit or earn eternal salvation through the strict observance of God's commandments." As anyone who has tried it will testify, legalism is indeed a yoke of bondage that is impossible to bear, especially given man's inherited sinful nature.

Personal Reflections

What was the most surprising or interesting thing that occurred to you as you studied this particular lesson about the Hebrew name יְשׁוּעַ *Yeshua*?

The Greek verb ἐλευθερόω *eleutheroō, to free,* has powerful ramifications in the life of the believer. How has Yeshua set you free in your life? Have you ever suffered under a mistaken, legalistic perspective of God's commandments – even the New Testament ones? Have you ever been in bondage to sinful practices, desires or motives?   Chances are, if you are anything like the rest of humanity, you've suffered from *both* – maybe both at once! Take a moment to write a thank-you letter to our LORD for freeing you from such enslavements (even if He's still in the midst of helping you work through some of these things right now. We're all a work in progress!).

Lesson 7

A composite meaning of the name *Yeshua*

*Christ and the pauper / Healing of the
blind man*, 2009, A.N. Mironov

*Open thou mine eyes,
that I may behold
wondrous things
out of Thy Law.*

Psalm 119:18 KJV

Lesson 7:
A composite meaning
of the name *Yeshua*

We've arrived at the final lesson of this book. Here's where you'll get the chance to compile all that you've learned about the name *Yeshua* over the past six lessons to create a composite meaning of His name.

We'll begin with a review exercise on the following pages. You'll fill in the blanks as you recall all that was taught in the prior lessons. If you need to look back, please do. Take your time. Enjoy it.

This is *not* a final exam, so, *please, no pressure*. This exercise is not intended to test your memory skills or your general comprehension. It is offered as a great opportunity for the Holy Spirit to bring back to mind all of the wonderful things you saw in the previous lessons (and probably forgot due to the constant flood of new information). We hope this review will provide an opportunity for the kind of spiritual refreshment that you can only get from a *second* look at these powerful, individual revelations – now that you've got the whole picture.

Cumulative Review Exercise

Please fill in the blanks. We have provided the page number reference for each question so that you may easily go back and find all the answers.

1 The name *Jesus* in Hebrew is *Yeshua.* What is the translation (meaning) of *Yeshua* in Hebrew? (page 16, paragraph 2)

____

2 The name Jesus in Hebrew is spelled using our alphabet as *Yeshua* or *Jeshua.* It's a newer, shorter form of an older name. What is that older name? (page 16, paragraph 2)

____

3 List at least 10 roles of Messiah Yeshua that were foreshadowed in the lives of the many men named *Yeshua* in the Old Testament. For example: "Mediator of a new covenant," "Teacher of God's Torah," etc. (pages 42-44)

____

____

____

____

____

____

____

____

____

　　　　Lesson 7: A composite meaning of the name *Yeshua*

4 One of the Hebrew roots of Yeshua's name is the verbal root **י.שׁ.ע** *yasha*. What is its core meaning? (page 50) ___________________________

5 List at least 7 different ways that the verb *yasha* is translated in Scripture (page 51)

____

____

____

____

____

____

____

6 The Hebrew root letters of *yasha* were brought directly into the Greek New Testament via the word *hoshana* (*hosanna*). What does *hoshana* mean? (page 62, paragraph 2) _______________________

7 *Hoshana Rabbah* is the "Great Save Now," that famous Great Day, the seventh day of the Feast of Tabernacles. On this day, who were the people of Israel traditionally praying for to come and save them? _______________________ (page 63, paragraph 1)

8 What three Jewish cultural and Biblical references to the Messiah were shouted by the crowd during the historical triumphal entry of Yeshua? (page 67, commentary)

____

____

____

9 *Hoshana Rabbah* is a day of crying out for rain – not just for physical water, but for the Holy Spirit. Yeshua claimed to be the fountain of the Holy Spirit on the day of *Hoshana Rabbah* when He claimed to be the source of what? (page 64, paragraph 1)

____

10 The Greek word σῴζω *sozo* is prominently connected with the events surrounding the naming of the infant Yeshua. What is *sozo's* core meaning? (page 75, paragraph 2)

____

11 List at least 10 ways that the Bible translates the word *sozo*. (Pages 79-80)

____

____

____

____

____

____

____

____

12 The Greek word ἐλευθερόω *eleutherŏō* is one possible Greek equivalent for the Hebrew verb *yasha*. What is the core meaning of *eleutherŏō*? (page 87, paragraph 4)

____

13 List at least 2 other ways that the word *eleutherŏō* may be translated. (page 88)

____

____

Make a "word cloud"

A fun way to visualize the nuanced uses and meanings of a term is to make a word cloud. At the center, you write the word you are studying. (We have already written *Yeshua* across the center of these two pages.) Then, you write as many related meanings as you can around the central word. Go back to the previous review exercise and scan the answers you wrote in the blanks. Using those answers as inspiration, write as many titles and definitions of *Yeshua* as you can, filling up any empty space below. You can use brightly colored markers if you like, or just a simple pen or pencil. We've already written some examples on the page to get you started.

living water

Teacher of Torah

defender

Son of David

liberator

builder of Jerusalem

*Therefore God also highly exalted Him,
and gave to Him the name which is above every name;
that at the name of Jesus every knee should bow,
of those in heaven, those on earth, and those under the earth,
and that every tongue should confess that Jesus Christ is Lord,
to the glory of God the Father.*

Philippians 2:9-11, WEB

          Lesson 7: A composite meaning of the name *Yeshua*

Personal Reflections

Reflecting on the word cloud you created on the previous pages, write a paragraph about the full meaning of the name יֵשׁוּעַ *Yeshua*. If you are part of a class studying this workbook together, share your paragraph with the rest of the group.

Other Books

by James T. and Lisa M. Cummins

Other Books
by James T. and Lisa M. Cummins

Messiah's Alphabet Book 1:
A workbook for learning how to read, write and pronounce the letters of the Hebrew alphabet

The first book in the *Messiah's Alphabet* Biblical Hebrew language series introduces the Hebrew alphabet to those with no prior knowledge of Hebrew. The student is shown how to draw simple "stick figure" shapes for each letter, and then learns the sound and name of each letter in a fun and friendly manner. The book gradually introduces some of the most frequently used Hebrew words in the Bible, gently assisting the reader in learning to recognize and pronounce each one. Audio files of every lesson available.

Available through online book retailers

Messiah's Alphabet Book 2:
Building a Biblical Vocabulary

The second book in the *Messiah's Alphabet* Biblical Hebrew language series, this workbook teaches basic Hebrew grammar on topics such as the definite article "<u>the</u>", the conjunction "<u>and</u>," plural nouns, adjectives and possessives for singular nouns. Guided readings of short Scripture passages are included throughout. Fun, simple exercises with all answers are provided. Puzzles, riddles and tear-out "flashcard" pages are included. Intended for students who have completed Book 1 or who have a solid working knowledge of the Hebrew alphabet and are able to phonetically "sound out" Hebrew words. Audio files of every lesson available.

Available through online book retailers

Other Books by James T. and Lisa M. Cummins

Messiah's Alphabet Book 3:
More Grammar for Biblical Hebrew

The third book in the *Messiah's Alphabet* Biblical Hebrew language series covers topics such as participles, prepositions (standalone and inseparable), prepositions with pronominal suffixes, and construct chains (word pairs). Each lesson introduces plenty of new Biblical Hebrew vocabulary. Continuing in the same fun and friendly style as the other books in the series, the workbook contains cartoons, jokes, puzzles, flashcard pages, and answers to all exercises. Audio files of vocabulary from every lesson are available.

Available through online book retailers

Messiah's Alphabet Book 4:
Verbs and More Grammar for Biblical Hebrew

The fourth book in the *Messiah's Alphabet* Biblical Hebrew language series covers verbs (roots, past tense, future tense, imperative and infinitive), the direct object marker, possessive suffixes for plural nouns, and the reversing *vav*. Each lesson introduces new Biblical Hebrew vocabulary. Continuing in the same fun and friendly style as the other books in the series, the workbook contains cartoons, jokes, puzzles, flashcard pages, and answers to all exercises. The book also includes verb charts, which display the conjugations of frequently used verbs. Audio files of all newly introduced vocabulary are available.

Available through online book retailers

Other Books by James T. and Lisa M. Cummins

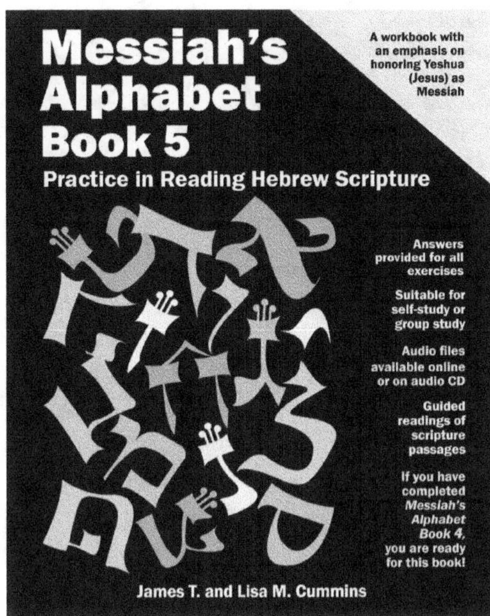

Messiah's Alphabet Book 5:
Practice in Reading Hebrew Scripture

This workbook allows the student who has completed Books 1 through 4 of the Biblical Hebrew language series to spread his or her wings and practice reading entire passages of Scripture, using mostly the vocabulary already taught in the series. Some new vocabulary is taught in this book, too, including tear-out flashcard pages, verb charts and glossary. Comparison tables of Christian, traditional Jewish and Messianic translations for every passage are included. Intriguing discussion questions explore selected Hebrew phrases. Complete answer keys with grammatical notations are included. Emphasis on Yeshua (Jesus) as Savior and LORD. Audio files of every lesson available.

Available through online book retailers

Messiah's Alphabet Word Study Series:
Shalom **– Fresh insights into the Biblical meanings of the Hebrew word** *shalom*

The Hebrew word *shalom* doesn't just mean "peace." At its core, *shalom* means "wholeness." That's why it's translated throughout the Bible with words like *health, welfare, peace, safety, prosperity, calm, success, well-being, close friendship, completeness,* and more. This word-study workbook takes the reader step by step through key Scripture passages which portray this powerful Hebrew word in its wide variety of meanings. For each verse of Scripture, the original Hebrew phrase containing the word *shalom* is shown, followed by the verse's full context in English. Various Bible translations of each verse are included for convenient cross-translation comparison. The last lesson of the book concludes with a brief New Testament word study on a Biblical Greek word for "peace" – *eirēnē* – demonstrating how the Hebraic concept of "*shalom* as wholeness" is carried into the New Testament.

Available through online book retailers

**Messiah's Alphabet:
Names Have Meaning**

This workbook explores the actual Hebrew meanings of the names of certain people mentioned in the Bible. Surprising discoveries will unfold as you connect the true meaning of each Hebrew name with its prophetic significance and fulfillment in Scripture. The hidden Hebrew meanings underlying the names of New Testament people are also brought to light. While a basic knowledge of the Hebrew and Greek alphabets may be helpful, it is not necessary, as all pronunciations are provided in transliteration form using the letters of the English alphabet. All answers are provided in the text. Audio files of every lesson available.

Available through online book retailers

**Messiah's Alphabet:
Places Have Meaning**

This workbook explores the actual Hebrew meanings of the names of certain places mentioned in the Bible. Surprising discoveries will unfold as you connect the true meaning of each Hebrew place name with its prophetic significance and fulfillment in Scripture. The hidden Hebrew meanings underlying the names of New Testament places are also brought to light. While a basic knowledge of the Hebrew and Greek alphabets may be helpful, it is not necessary, as all pronunciations are provided in transliteration form using the letters of the English alphabet. All answers are provided in the text. Audio files of every lesson available.

Available through online book retailers

Other Books by James T. and Lisa M. Cummins

Biblical Greek Book 1:
A workbook for learning how to read, write and pronounce the letters of the Greek alphabet

The first book in the *Biblical Greek* language series introduces the Greek alphabet to those with no prior knowledge of Greek. The student is shown how to draw simple "stick figure" shapes for each letter, and then learns the sound and name of each letter in a fun and friendly manner. The book gradually introduces some of the most frequently used Greek words in the New Testament, gently assisting the reader in learning to recognize and pronounce each one. Audio files of every lesson available.

Available through online book retailers

Biblical Greek Book 2:
Nouns and Cases

The second book in the *Biblical Greek* language series teaches Greek nouns (singular and plural forms) and the five cases (nominative, genitive, dative, accusative and vocative), as well as the Greek article in all its forms. Book 2 expands on the reader's basic knowledge of the "Top Twenty" most frequently used Greek nouns of the New Testament (whose nominative singular forms are taught in Book 1) while adding additional vocabulary. Easy English examples illustrate all Greek grammar principles, which are explained in straightforward, everyday language. Handy charts, tables, lists, flashcards and a glossary of all vocabulary are provided. Friendly, enlarged graphics are employed to teach stem letters and case endings. Actual New Testament Scripture is used in the examples and exercises, for which complete answer keys are included.

Available through online book retailers

God invented a calendar.
Now, you can learn all about it!

Did any New Testament events align with God's special "appointed times" of the Old Testament?

How do God's Old Testament holy days act as prophetic pictures and symbols of future events in the end times?

How does knowing the order of the Biblical months help clarify the order of events in the New Testament?

Don't worry if you've never heard of a Biblical calendar before... *Messiah's Calendar Book 1: Days, Weeks, Months and Years* offers a gentle introduction to the concepts of Biblical timekeeping, God's calendar, and God's appointed times – with an emphasis on their ultimate fulfillment in Messiah Yeshua (Jesus). Learn about God's definitions of the day, the week, the month and the year. Get familiar with the order of the Biblical months and see how it helps clarify the order of events in your New Testament. This book's educational illustrations and excellent graphics – packed with prophetic insights and historical information - make God's calendar easy to grasp.   The writing style and choice of vocabulary are sensitive to both Jewish and Gentile readers, so this book is suitable for churches and Messianic congregations alike.

Other great features include:

- **Educational illustrations throughout**

- **Packed with Biblical insights**

- **Listed Scriptures are fully "typed out" for convenience in classroom study**

- **Brief descriptions of all feasts and fasts**

- **Easy explanations of any Hebrew or Greek terms, with simple phonetic pronunciations. (Prior knowledge of Hebrew or Greek is not necessary.)**

- **Additional resources in the back, including graphics, teachings and glossary/index**

- **Excellent for either group or individual study**

Available through online book retailers.

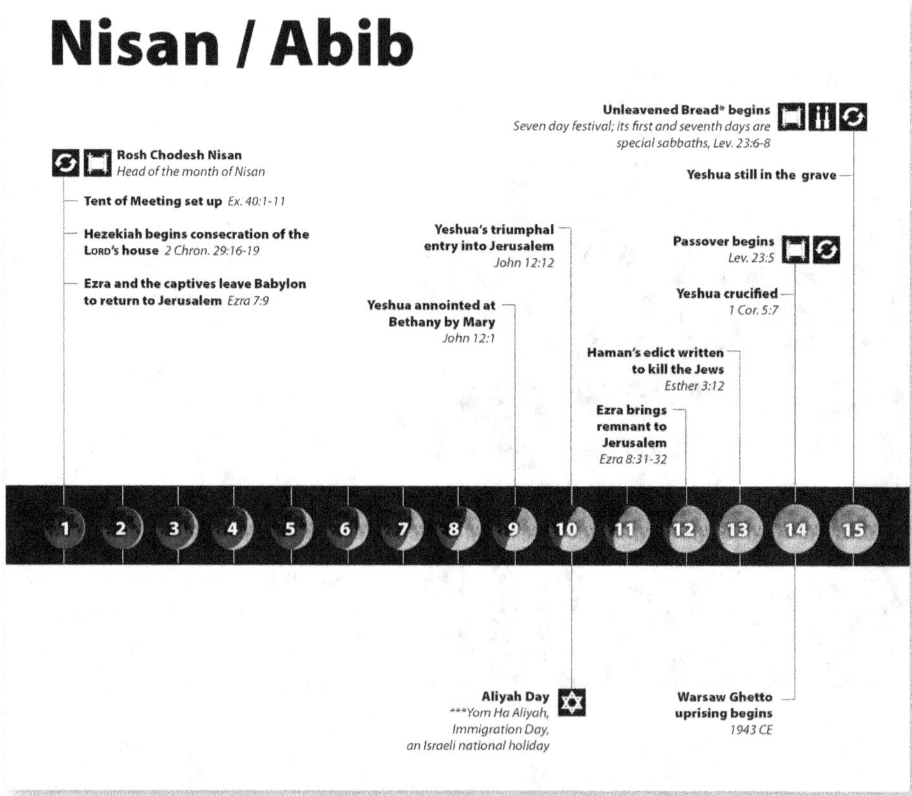

You'll enjoy the clear, easy to use graphics – portraying the date of every event mentioned in Scripture... as well as the dates of key historical events which are not mentioned in the Bible.

   Other books by James T. and Lisa M. Cummins

God established His feasts.
Now, you can learn all about them!

Which major events of Jesus' life align with God's special appointed times of the Old Testament?

How do God's Old Testament holy days act as prophetic pictures and symbols of future events in the end times?

The New Testament suggests that believers observed the feasts for decades after the resurrection of Jesus. Why did they?

Can one still celebrate God's appointed times today – by grace, through faith – in a way that magnifies and glorifies Jesus?

Find the answers to these questions and more in *Messiah's Calendar Book 2: The Feasts of the LORD*. Each chapter is devoted to one of the seven appointed times of the Lord described in Leviticus 23, and contains educational charts, helpful graphics, beautiful illustrations and often-overlooked Biblical insights. God's seven appointed times are explored in depth, including their symbolism in prophecy and their fulfillment in the New Testament ministry of Jesus. For those readers who feel God's leading to learn how to observe the feasts, optional "observance" sections contain suggested prayers, Scripture readings, songs, recipes and children's crafts. Easy explanations of any Greek or Hebrew terms are provided, along with simple phonetic pronunciations, so that prior knowledge of Hebrew or Greek is not necessary.

Available through online book retailers.

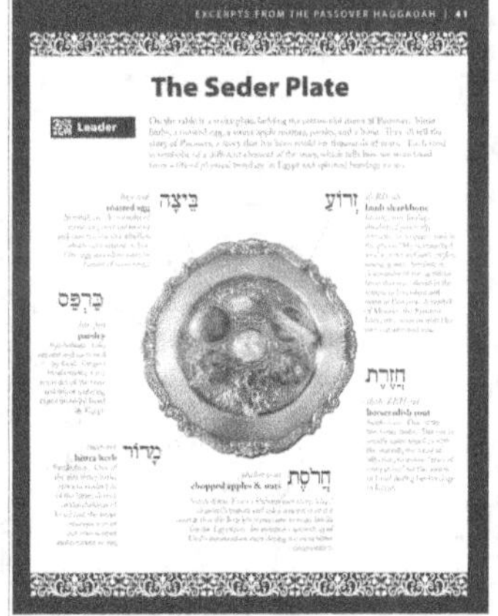

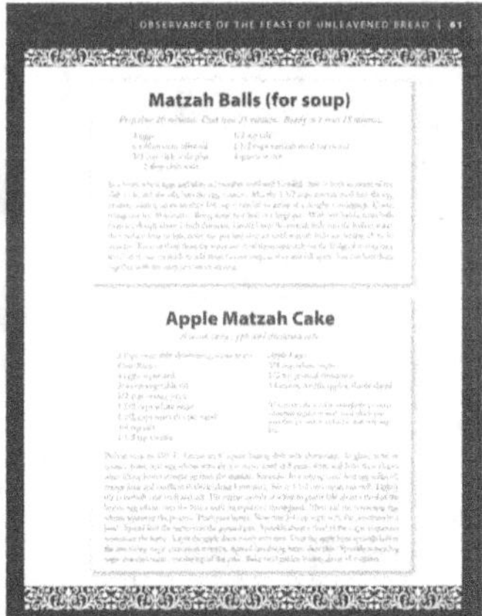

"Observance" sections at the end of each chapter suggest optional prayers, Scripture readings, songs, recipes and children's crafts

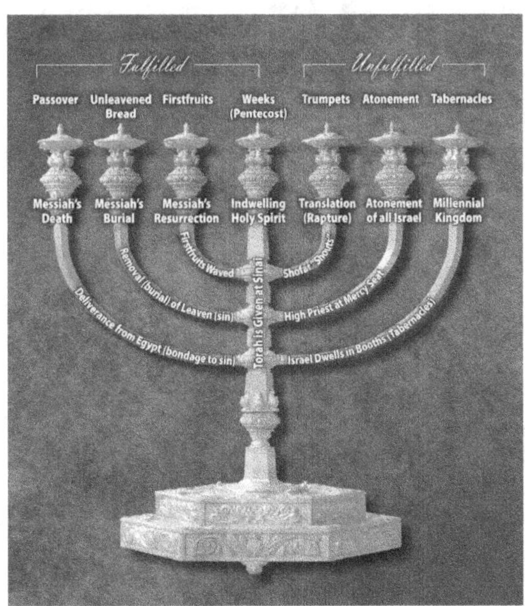

Beautiful graphics present God's feasts simply and elegantly.

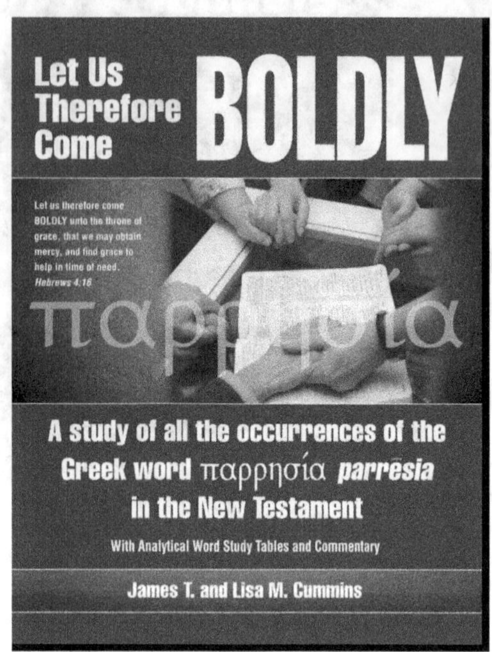

Let Us Therefore Come BOLDLY:
A study of all the occurrences of the Greek word *parresia* **in the New Testament**

This book leads the reader through all the occurrences of the Greek word for "boldness" in the New Testament. Throughout the study, the various meanings of this deep and wonderful Greek word are uncovered, along with practical applications for the believer's life. Graphic tables and insightful commentary make it easy for the student to understand the significance of every separate mention of the Greek word *parresia* – even if the student has no knowledge of the Greek language.

Available through online book retailers

<u>Other Books by James T. and Lisa M. Cummins</u>

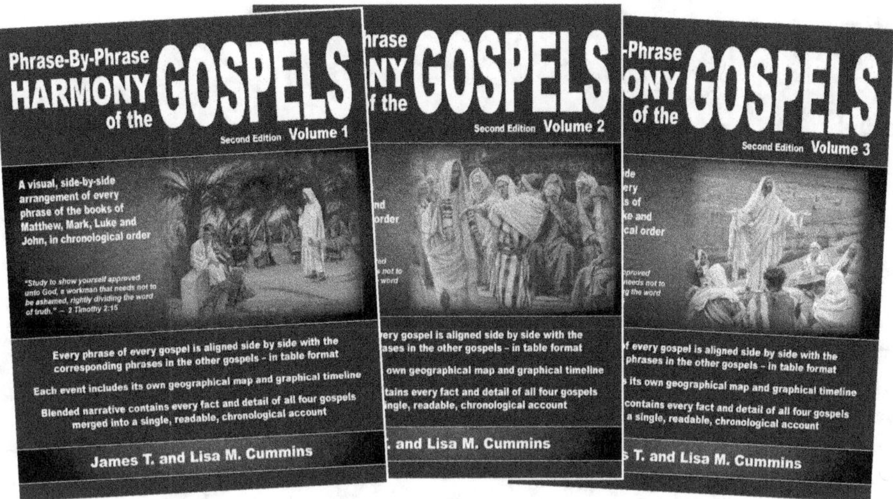

This three-volume set provides a visual, side-by-side arrangement of every phrase of the books of Matthew, Mark, Luke and John, in chronological order. Every phrase of every gospel is aligned side by side with the corresponding phrases in the other gospels, in table format. Each event includes its own geographical map and graphical timeline. Included blended narrative contains every fact and detail of all four gospels merged into a single, readable, chronological account.
See the following pages for a sample of the interior layout.

How is the *Phrase-By-Phrase Harmony of the Gospels* different from traditional harmonies?

Have you ever attempted to study a particular event recorded in the books of Matthew, Mark, Luke and John – but then got confused about the exact order of the details because of all the "flipping back and forth" in your Bible that you had to do? If you're like us, maybe you thought the whole process was unnecessarily awkward and difficult. You only wanted to get the full picture of the event. But in order to do that, you had to try to remember every detail from each gospel – and then be able to put all the facts in the right order! It's really hard to do. It's like being on a jury and having to recall every detail of the witness testimonies – in the right order – to figure out what actually happened.

Throughout history, eminent Bible scholars have attempted to compile the four gospels into a single account to make studying the gospels easier. The scholarly term for such a compilation is a *harmony*. Such traditional harmonies put the *complete paragraphs* describing an event from Matthew in one column, then the *complete paragraphs* from Mark's testimony in another column (side by side with the Matthew column), then Luke's column of paragraphs next to Mark's, and finally John's column at the end. But none of those harmonies ever provided the level of granular detail we were after. What *we* wanted was to be able to see *every individual fact* compared side by side on a phrase-by-phrase basis. For years, we scoured the world for *that* type of harmony and never did find one. Finally, we gave up and wrote our own.

While we were at it, we decided to address *another* problem we always face in our Bible study: the challenge of remembering *where* and *when* each event of the gospels occurred. We included a timeline and a map with every event, which helped us to visualize the whole string of events as a continuous narrative across space and time. To our delight, we discovered that these timelines and maps also served to refresh our memories between study sessions.

After making all those additions, it seemed to make sense to go ahead and add one more thing: a smooth, blended narrative combining all the facts for each event. The blended narrative may be found at the end of each section.

So that's how our harmony turned out a bit different from other harmonies. We've found it to be both a helpful reference tool and an anointed devotional guide. We hope you enjoy studying from it as much as we do.

– Jim and Lisa

<u>Sample section from the *Phrase-By-Phrase Harmony of the Gospels*</u>

Modular design allows you to focus your attention on just one gospel event per section.

Graphical timeline on every section helps you recall what happened before and anticipate what's coming up.

Chronological Notes provide insightful commentary on the historical or cultural significance of any time references

Geographical notes with map on every section help you visualize where each event occurs. Historical and archaeological notes are provided where applicable.

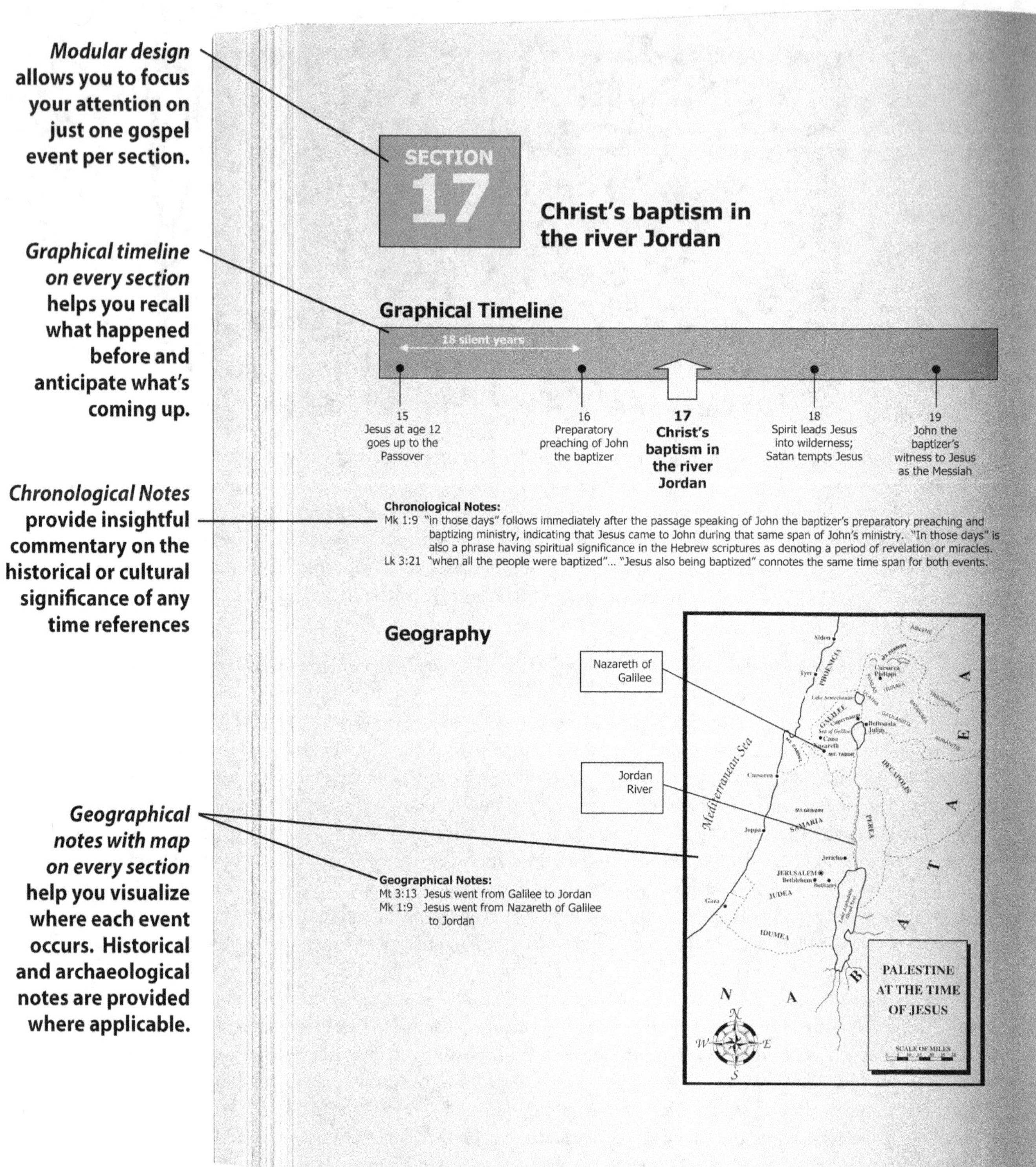

Facing page layout keeps timelines and maps physically adjacent to (or within the distance of a few pages of) the relevant gospel texts, for ease of reference.

Other books by James T. and Lisa M. Cummins

Sample section from the *Phrase-By-Phrase Harmony of the Gospels*

Phrase-By-Phrase Harmonized Table

Matthew 3: 13-17	Mark 1: 9-11	Luke 3: 21-22	John
	9a And it came to pass *in those days,*	21a Now *when all the people were baptized,* it came to pass,	
13a Then cometh Jesus from **Galilee**	9b that Jesus came from **Nazareth of Galilee.**		
13b to **Jordan** unto John, to be baptized of him.			
14 But John forbad him, saying, I have need to be baptized of thee, and comest thou to me?			
15a And Jesus answering said unto him, Suffer it to be so now: for thus it becometh us to fulfil all righteousness.			
15b Then he suffered him.			
16a And Jesus, when he was baptized	9c and was baptized of John in **Jordan**.	21a that Jesus also being baptized,	
16b went up straightway out of the water:	10a and straightway coming up out of the water.		
		21b and praying,	
16c and, lo, the heavens were opened unto him,	10b he saw the heavens opened,	21c the heaven was opened,	
16d he saw the Spirit of God descending like a dove, and lighting upon him:	10c and the Spirit like a dove descending upon him:	22a And the Holy Ghost descended in a bodily shape like a dove upon him,	
17 And lo a voice from heaven, saying, This is my beloved Son, in whom I am well pleased.	11 And there came a voice from heaven, saying, Thou art my beloved Son, in whom I am well pleased.	22b and a voice from heaven, which said, Thou art my beloved Son; in thee I am well pleased.	

Blended Narrative

In those days, when all the people were being baptized by John, Jesus came from Nazareth of Galilee to Jordan to be baptized by John. But John tried to prevent Him, saying, "I need to be baptized by you, and you come to me?" Jesus answered him, "Permit it for now, for in this way it is fitting for us to fulfill all righteousness." Then he permitted Him. When Jesus was baptized by John in the Jordan, He came straightway up out of the water, and praying, he saw the heavens opened to him, and saw the Holy Spirit of God descending in a bodily shape like a dove and landing on Him. And there came a voice from heaven, saying, "You are my beloved Son; in you I am well pleased. This is my beloved Son, in whom I am well pleased."

(Here it is possible that God spoke both to Jesus and to those gathered at the Jordan at the same time, which accounts for the different modes of address – 2nd person singular speaks directly to Jesus, while 3rd person singular speaks about Jesus, as an audible witness to those present.)

In the table above, ***bold italic*** print indicates a time/chronological reference; **<u>bold underline</u>** print indicates a place/geographical reference.

Phrase-by-phrase table lets you compare every phrase of Scripture from each of the four gospels at a glance. Underscored and bolded typefaces highlight geographical references; italicized text highlights time references.

Blended narrative provides a single account that smoothly merges every factual detail from all four gospels in chronological order.

Authors' commentary clarifies difficult or problematic texts when necessary.

Lists of Scripture References at the end of each volume provide an exhaustive index in five sorted lists. Four lists are filtered and sorted by individual book (Matthew, Mark, Luke or John), making it easy to locate a particular verse. The fifth list is sorted by Section number (i.e., by event) and displays all four contributing gospel references.

<u>Fiction by James T. and Lisa M. Cummins</u>

Orchard Hill
A personal Appalachian triumph

It is a time of economic desperation.
When Raybun returns to the Kentucky homeplace after fighting in the Second World War, he is dismayed to discover the entire region suffering in extreme poverty resulting from economic changes beyond anyone's control. Now, Raybun must find a way to help his family and community. Through a series of small miracles and a growing, persistent faith, Raybun and his friends are able to bring restoration to the broken community, and find love along the way.

Available through online book retailers under author names James T. and Lisa M. Cummins and pseudonyms Raybun and Penelope Bowland

Dr. Dalton
A continuing personal Appalachian triumph

In this sequel to *Orchard Hill*, Dr. Dalton Bowland works as a family practitioner at a lucrative, multi-specialty practice in an upper-middle-class suburb of Columbus, Ohio. According to his colleagues – and his fat bank account – his career has been fabulously successful thus far. Why, then, does he feel so uninspired? Quitting his job at the Ohio practice, Dr. Bowland makes a long-overdue visit to the rural Kentucky medical clinics established decades earlier by his deceased parents' charitable foundation. The shock of what he discovers there, along with the desperate needs of the people he meets, will change his life forever.

Available through online book retailers

　　　　Other books by James T. and Lisa M. Cummins

Fiction by James T. and Lisa M. Cummins

Homesteader

It's 1957, and thirteen-year-old Jimmy dreams of homesteading a piece of land just like he's seen the pioneers do on his favorite TV show. As soon as he finds the perfect spot to build a homestead, he gets caught trespassing on an old man's property.   It's just the first of many hard lessons about the realities of life. After years of hard work and patience, Jimmy gradually begins to have some success. Throughout life's tragedies and triumphs, he learns the value of enduring friendship.

Available through online book retailers